APP for Reading and Writing

Year 2

Gillian Howell

Contents

Pearson Education Limited, a company incorporated in England and Wales, having its registered office at Edinburgh Gate, Harlow, Essex, CM20 2JE. Registered company number: 872828

www.pearsonschools.co.uk

Text © Pearson Education Limited 2010

First published 2010

14 13 12

10 9 8 7 6 5 4 3 2

British Library Cataloguing in Publication Data

A catalogue record for this book is available from the British Library.

ISBN 978 0 435 04151 9

Literacy consultant: Anne Derry

Typeset by Zed

Illustrated by Russ Daff **10**, **12**, **13**, **15**, **16**; Anna Godwin **22**, **23**; Gary Joynes **43**, **44**, **45**, **47**; Robin Lawrie **31**, **32**, **34**, **35**, **37**; Matt Ward **55**, **58**, **65**, **66**, **68**.

Cover illustration by Clive Goodyer © Pearson Education Limited

Printed and bound in the UK by Henry Ling Ltd

Acknowledgements

The publisher would like to thank Longcot and Fernham CE Primary School for its invaluable help with producing children's writing samples for this book.

The publisher would like to thank the following for permission to use their copyright material.

Text

Reading and Writing Assessment Guidelines (on pages 7–8) © Crown copyright 2009, reproduced under the terms of the Click-Use Licence.

On my way from school by Roger Stevens © Roger Stevens. Published by Rabbit Press. Used by kind permission of the author.

Photographs

(Key: b-bottom; c-centre; l-left; r-right; t-top)

Alamy Images: Christopher Jones **53t**, David Crausby **64r**, Tracy Ferrero **64cr**; Photolibrary.com: Ingram Publishing **64cl**; Shutterstock: Ragnarock **64l**

Penguin Books UK Limited: cover of *Each Peach Pear Plum* by Janet and Allan Ahlberg, published by Viking. Used by permission of Penguin Books UK Limited **53b**; cover of *Funnybones* by Janet and Allan Ahlberg, published by Penguin. Used by permission of Penguin Book UK Limited **54l**; cover of *The Jolly Postman* by Janet and Allan Ahlberg, published by Viking. Used by permission of Penguin Books UK Limited **54r**; cover of *Please Mrs. Butler* by Janet and Allan Ahlberg, published by Kestrel. Used by permission of Penguin Books UK Limited **54c**.

Every effort has been made to contact copyright holders of material reproduced in this book. Any omissions will be rectified in subsequent printings if notice is given to the publishers.

APP for Reading and Writing has been developed to help you accurately assess your pupils' progress and attainment in reading and writing skills, using texts and questions designed to elicit evidence for specific assessment points. This Year 2 file contains six tasks, covering the Assessment Foci for National Curriculum Levels 2 and 3.

How to use this book

The tasks in this book are designed to support the periodic assessment that is a key part of the 'Assessing Pupils' Progress' (APP) evidence gathering. The tasks help you gather evidence to support your own professional understanding of each child's level of achievement. The tasks should help you form a good understanding of the National Curriculum level at which children are working. They have been written to work in conjunction with, and should be used alongside, the QCDA and National Strategy APP Assessment Guidance charts and the Standards files. Copies of the Assessment Guidance charts are included on pages 7 and 8.

Gathering assessment evidence to address Assessment Foci

The Assessment Guidance charts on pages 7 and 8 outline the Assessment Foci for Reading and Writing, all of which are covered by the tasks in this book. The chart on the top of page 6 gives an overview of this coverage. Where a child is not demonstrating the reading and / or writing evidence expected at Level 2 in these tasks, you may want to find an equivalent task from the Year 1 book to collect evidence across Levels 1 and 2. The tasks cover the same Assessment Foci although the genre of the stimulus pieces may differ.

Using the tasks in the classroom

There are six tasks in this book, which can be integrated into your school's literacy planning. The tasks are based on stimulus pieces from a variety of fiction and non-fiction text types. Each of the tasks allows you to collect evidence for both reading and writing. The tasks may also provide evidence about pupils' attainment and progress in speaking and listening. We recommend that children carry out the reading activity first, so that they are familiar with the stimulus piece before completing the writing activity. Each task is designed to take approximately 30 minutes to complete. The tasks will support your evidence gathering, but will not be the sole basis for your judgements about pupils' achievement.

Teacher Sheets

Each task has a Teacher Sheet offering an overview of the task, the key concepts it targets and the related Renewed Framework unit and objectives it covers.

Reading tasks

To support you in gathering evidence for AF1, running records have been provided for the fiction stimulus texts. Further guidance on using the running records can be found on pages 4–5.

For reading AFs 2–7, you can choose between working with a small group for guided reading, or asking children to read and answer the questions independently. The guided reading questions are supplied on the Teacher Sheet for each task. You might like to use these to collect evidence through open discussion, in which case you can use the assessment guidance sheet to capture notes about individual oral responses. If you would rather ask children to work independently, the questions and space to answer them are provided on the photocopiable sheets for each task.

The bold questions on the Teacher Sheet are those that are included on the photocopiable Reading Response Sheets.

For both guided and independent reading, the questions focus on two or three AFs, and the assessment guidance sheet gives you examples of the kind of responses children may give, and the level this would indicate.

Writing tasks

For writing, children complete a number of short-answer questions and a longer writing activity. Real examples of children's work are provided, along with notes to help you assess children's work for all the Assessment Foci. It should be noted that responses can vary within a level depending on the type of writing pupils are asked to do (e.g. some may not do as well with narrative as they do with report). Therefore, attainment and progress for any pupil should not be expected to be totally linear.

Making assessment judgements

No single task can determine that a child is low, secure or high Level 2 or Level 3. However, observing a child working on several tasks over a period of time will provide evidence of their functioning at a particular level for reading and writing and should also give an indication of their security within that level. You will need to combine the evidence that these tasks give you with your day-to-day knowledge of a child's performance to decide how consistently the evidence fits the criteria in the Assessment Focus in order to determine whether the child's performance at that level is 'low', 'secure' or 'high'. You should also gather evidence for reading and writing from other subject areas.

A child may prove to be at different levels for different Assessment Foci, and be at a different level for reading than for writing. When you highlight the areas at which they are working on the assessment grids, you may see a 'spiky profile'; you can use this to inform your future planning to fill in any gaps in children's knowledge or skills by referring to the learning objectives that underpin that particular Assessment Focus.

Consistency and moderation

The example answers provided in this book are designed to help you gauge the level at which the children in your class are performing. However, these examples are provided as a guide only and professional judgement must be used when reviewing the evidence and making consistent judgements about children's attainment. The examples cannot cover all the different ways in which different children may respond. When you are reviewing the evidence from these tasks, along with other evidence, to make a level judgement, it is good practice to confer with a colleague who knows the children's performance in literacy to corroborate your judgement.

What to do next

At the end of each Task, 'next steps' guidance is given about what teachers might do next in terms of planning for teaching and learning for the relevant AFs, referenced to the appropriate learning objectives. This guidance also points to other assessments within the book that cover those AFs.

Running records

Running records can be used periodically to identify gaps in a pupil's learning and to inform planning and teaching. In this way they can support 'Assessing Pupils' Progress' (APP).

Running records should contribute to a wide range of evidence gathered about how each pupil is progressing so that reliable judgements relating to national standards can be made.

For your running record assessments, you will need: a running record sheet; the corresponding Task text; pencil / pen; a quiet space.

Before reading:
- Ask the pupil to sit beside you.
- Record the pupil's name and the date of the assessment.
- Give the pupil the text and explain that you want him or her to read aloud.
- Explain that you are going to see how well he or she can manage without prompts from you.
- Introduce the text by looking at the title of the story.

When you and the pupil are ready, ask the pupil to start reading. In some cases, the text for the running record starts from the second or third paragraph so that the pupil can settle into reading before the assessment begins.

Marking the running record
Use the reading symbols outlined on the bottom of the running record to mark the text as the pupil reads. Note the reading strategies used by the pupil in the column 'Strategies used'. At the end of the running record assessment, count the number of miscues (errors) the pupil made and record the total number in the 'Miscues total' box. Evidence gathered during the assessment about how frequently the pupil self-corrected and what reading strategies he or she used should help to identify any gaps in the pupil's learning and lead to informed planning and teaching.

Using the evidence gathered
Once the total number of miscues has been counted, determine the percentage accuracy rate using the tables at the bottom of the sheet. Simply find the number of miscues in the top row of the correct table to find the corresponding accuracy rate in the bottom row.

Using the analysis to inform teaching
To inform teaching, analyse the pupil's self-corrections and errors by looking at the reading strategies he or she uses. These will help you to understand where they are in their reading and what they need to focus on in order to accurately decode the text and read for meaning (AF1).

For example, a running record where '**Ph**' (for phonic) is consistently noted indicates that the pupil is reliably using phonics to decode each word. The accuracy rate will give you an idea of the pupil's fluency; however, the next steps in planning and teaching should include assessing how well the pupil reads for meaning.

A running record where '**G**' (for graphic) is frequently noted indicates that the pupil may be focusing on the letters of a word rather than thinking about whether his or her reading sounds right and makes sense. For example, the pupil might substitute a word that looks similar, but does not make sense in the sentence.

Alternatively, '**S**' (for syntactic) indicates that the pupil suggests a grammatically sensible alternative to the word so that it sounds right, but he or she is misreading the text. Similarly, '**C**' (for contextual) indicates that the pupil is thinking about the meaning of the word and will substitute a word that makes sense in context but, again, he or she is misreading the text. Both syntactic and contextual reading strategies indicate that the pupil can read for meaning, but may need to practise decoding of the text.

Assessment Foci covered by the Year 2 tasks

● = Main AFs   ○ = Other AFs

READING

	AF1	AF2	AF3	AF4	AF5	AF6	AF7	
Task 1: Lost and Found!	●	●	●					
Task 2: On my way from school	○			○	●	●		
Task 3: Mother Holle	●	●	○			●		
Task 4: Electrical Circuits	○	●	●	●	●			
Task 5: Allan Ahlberg	○	●	●	○				
Task 6: Birds in the City	○	●		●		●		

WRITING

	AF1	AF2	AF3	AF4	AF5	AF6	AF7	AF8
Task 1: Lost and Found!	●			○	○	●	●	○
Task 2: On my way from school	●	●	●			○	●	
Task 3: Mother Holle	●	●	●	○		○	●	
Task 4: Electrical Circuits			○		●	●	●	○
Task 5: Allan Ahlberg	○	●				●	●	○
Task 6: Birds in the City			●	●	●	○	○	

Renewed Framework for Literacy Reading and Writing Objectives covered by the Year 2 tasks

5. Word recognition: decoding (reading) and encoding (spelling)
   5.1   Read independently and with increasing fluency longer and less familiar texts
   5.2   Spell with increasing accuracy and confidence, drawing on word recognition and knowledge of word structure, and spelling patterns
   5.3   Know how to tackle unfamiliar words that are not completely decodable
   5.5   Read high and medium frequency words independently and automatically

7. Understanding and interpreting texts
   7.1   Draw together ideas and information from across a whole text, using simple signposts in the text
   7.2   Give some reasons why things happen or characters change
   7.3   Explain organisational features of texts
   7.5   Explore how particular words are used, including words and expressions with similar meanings

8. Engaging with and responding to texts
   8.2   Engage with books through exploring and enacting interpretations
   8.3   Explain their reactions to texts, commenting on important aspects

9. Creating and shaping texts
   9.1   Draw on knowledge and experience of texts in deciding and planning what and how to write
   9.3   Maintain consistency in non-narrative, including purpose and tense
   9.4   Make adventurous word and language choices appropriate to the style and purpose of the text
   9.5   Select from different presentational features to suit particular writing purposes on paper

10. Text structure and organisation
   10.1 Use planning to establish clear sections for writing
   10.2 Use appropriate language to make sections hang together

11. Sentence structure and punctuation
   11.1 Write simple and compound sentences; begin to use subordination in relation to time / reason
   11.2 Compose sentences using tense consistently (present and past)

Task	Renewed Framework objectives covered
Task 1: Lost and Found!	5.2, 5.3, 5.5, 7.2. 8.3, 9.3, 10.1
Task 2: On my way from school	7.1, 7.2, 7.5, 8.3, 9.1, 9.4
Task 3: Mother Holle	5.1, 7.2, 8.2, 9.1, 9.4, 10.2
Task 4: Electrical Circuits	5.2, 7.1, 7.3, 9.1, 9.3, 9.5, 11.1
Task 5: Allan Ahlberg	5.2, 7.1, 7.3, 8.3, 9.3, 9.4, 11.1
Task 6: Birds in the City	7.1, 7.3, 9.3, 9.5, 10.1, 11.2

QCDA Reading Assessment Guidelines: Levels 2 and 3

	AF1 – use a range of strategies, including accurate decoding of text, to read for meaning	AF2 – understand, describe, select or retrieve information, events or ideas from texts and use quotation and reference to text	AF3 – deduce, infer or interpret information, events or ideas from texts	AF4 – identify and comment on the structure and organisation of texts, including grammatical and presentational features at text level	AF5 – explain and comment on writers' use of language, including grammatical and literary features at word and sentence level	AF6 – identify and comment on writers' purposes and viewpoints, and the overall effect of the text on the reader	AF7 – relate texts to their social, cultural and historical traditions
L3	**In most reading:** • range of strategies used mostly effectively to read with fluency, understanding and expression	**In most reading:** • simple, most obvious points identified though there may also be some misunderstanding, e.g. about information from different places in the text • some comments include quotations from or references to text, but not always relevant, e.g. often retelling or paraphrasing sections of the text rather than using it to support comment	**In most reading:** • straightforward inference based on a single point of reference in the text, e.g. 'he was upset because it says "he was crying"' • responses to text show meaning established at a literal level e.g. '"walking good" means "walking carefully"' or based on personal speculation e.g. a response based on what they personally would be feeling rather than feelings of character in the text	**In most reading:** • a few basic features of organisation at text level identified, with little or no linked comment, e.g. 'it tells about all the different things you can do at the zoo'	**In most reading:** • a few basic features of writer's use of language identified, but with little or no comment, e.g. 'there are lots of adjectives' or 'he uses speech marks to show there are lots of people there'	**In most reading:** • comments identify main purpose, e.g. 'the writer doesn't like violence' • express personal response but with little awareness of writer's viewpoint or effect on reader, e.g. 'she was just horrible like my nan is sometimes'	**In most reading:** • some simple connections between texts identified, e.g. similarities in plot, topic, or books by same author, about same characters • recognition of some features of the context of texts, e.g. historical setting, social or cultural background
L2	**In some reading:** • range of key words read on sight • unfamiliar words decoded using appropriate strategies, e.g. blending sounds • some fluency and expression, e.g. taking account of punctuation, speech marks	**In some reading:** • some specific, straightforward information recalled, e.g. names of characters, main ingredients • generally clear idea of where to look for information, e.g. about characters, topics	**In some reading:** • simple, plausible inference about events and information, using evidence from text, e.g. how a character is feeling, what makes a plant grow • comments based on textual cues, sometimes misunderstood	**In some reading:** • some awareness of use of features of organisation, e.g. beginning and ending of story, types of punctuation	**In some reading:** • some effective language choices noted, e.g. '"slimy" is a good word there' • some familiar patterns of language identified, e.g. once upon a time; first, next, last	**In some reading:** • some awareness that writers have viewpoints and purposes, e.g. 'it tells you how to do something', 'she thinks it's not fair' • simple statements about likes and dislikes in reading, sometimes with reasons	**In some reading:** • general features of a few text types identified, e.g. information books, stories, print media • some awareness that books are set in different times and places
BL							
IE							

Overall assessment (tick one box only) Low 2 ☐ Secure 2 ☐ High 2 ☐ Low 3 ☐ Secure 3 ☐ High 3 ☐

BL = 'Below Level'   IE = 'Insufficient Evidence'

QCDA Writing Assessment Guidelines: Levels 2 and 3

	AF5 – vary sentences for clarity, purpose and effect	AF6 – write with technical accuracy of syntax and punctuation in phrases, clauses and sentences	AF3 – organise and present whole texts effectively, sequencing and structuring information, ideas and events	AF4 – construct paragraphs and use cohesion within and between paragraphs	AF1 – write imaginative, interesting and thoughtful texts	AF2 – produce texts which are appropriate to task, reader and purpose	AF7 – select appropriate and effective vocabulary	AF8 – use correct spelling	Handwriting and presentation
L3	**In most writing:** • reliance mainly on simply structured sentences, variation with support, e.g. *some complex sentences* • *and, but, so* are the most common connectives, subordination occasionally • some limited variation in use of tense and verb forms, not always secure	**In most writing:** • straightforward sentences usually demarcated accurately with full stops, capital letters, question and exclamation marks • some, limited, use of speech punctuation • comma splicing evident, particularly in narrative	**In most writing:** • some attempt to organise ideas with related points placed next to each other • openings and closings usually signalled • some attempt to sequence ideas or material logically	**In most writing:** • some internal structure within sections of text *e.g. one-sentence paragraphs or ideas loosely organised* • within paragraphs/ sections, some links between sentences, *e.g. use of pronouns or of adverbials* • movement between paragraphs/sections sometimes abrupt or disjointed	**In most writing:** • some appropriate ideas and content included • some attempt to elaborate on basic information or events, *e.g. nouns expanded by simple adjectives* • attempt to adopt viewpoint, though often not maintained or inconsistent, *e.g. attitude expressed, but with little elaboration*	**In most writing:** • purpose established at a general level • main features of selected form sometimes signalled to the reader • some attempts at appropriate style, with attention to reader	**In most writing:** • simple, generally appropriate vocabulary used, limited in range • some words selected for effect or occasion	**In most writing:** • correct spelling of – some common grammatical function words – common content/ lexical words with more than one morpheme, including compound words • likely errors – *some inflected endings, e.g. past tense, comparatives, adverbs – some phonetically plausible attempts at content/lexical words*	**In most writing:** • legible style, shows accurate and consistent letter formation, sometimes joined
L2	**In some forms of writing:** • some variation in sentence openings, *e.g. not always starting with name or pronoun* • mainly simple sentences with *and* used to connect clauses • past and present tense generally consistent	**In some forms of writing:** • clause structure mostly grammatically correct • sentence demarcation with capital letters and full stops usually accurate • some accurate use of question and exclamation marks, and commas in lists	**In some forms of writing:** • some basic sequencing of ideas or material, *e.g. time-related words or phrases, line breaks, headings, numbers* • openings and/or closings sometimes signalled	**In some forms of writing:** • ideas in sections grouped by content, some linking by simple pronouns	**In some forms of writing:** • mostly relevant ideas and content, sometimes repetitive or sparse • some apt word choices create interest • brief comments, questions about events or actions suggest viewpoint	**In some forms of writing:** • some basic purpose established, *e.g. main features of story, report* • some appropriate features of the given form used • some attempts to adopt appropriate style	**In some forms of writing:** • simple, often speech-like vocabulary conveys relevant meanings • some adventurous word choices, *e.g. opportune use of new vocabulary*	**In some forms of writing:** • usually correct spelling of: – high frequency grammatical function words – common single-morpheme content/ lexical words • likely errors: – inflected endings, *e.g. past tense, plurals, adverbs* – phonetic attempts at vowel digraphs	**In some forms of writing:** • letters generally correctly shaped but inconsistencies in orientation, size and use of upper/lower case letters • clear letter formation, with ascenders and descenders distinguished, generally upper and lower case letters not mixed within words
BL									
IE									

Overall assessment (tick one box only) Low 2 ☐ Secure 2 ☐ High 2 ☐ Low 3 ☐ Secure 3 ☐ High 3 ☐   BL = 'Below Level' IE = 'Insufficient Evidence'

Task 1 Lost and Found!

Aims of this task

This task is designed to help you make judgements about children's performance in Reading **AF1, AF2** and **AF3** and Writing **AF1, AF6** and **AF7** (with opportunities to assess AF4, AF5 and AF8 as well). Children read and respond to a story in a familiar setting (a Do It Yourself shop) with a familiar theme (losing someone or something). They plan and write sentences for a beginning, middle and end of their own story.

Related Renewed Framework unit

Narrative Unit 1: Stories with familiar settings

Renewed Framework objectives

5.2, 5.3, 5.5, 7.2. 8.3, 9.3, 10.1

Key concepts

Reading
- read fluently with understanding and expression (AF1)
- identify key events and their sequence in the story (AF2)
- make inferences about why events happened and how characters feel, based on evidence in the story (AF3)

Writing
- use the story setting from reading to write a different story in the same setting (AF1)
- write sentences using capital letters to begin and accurate punctuation to end (AF6)
- use appropriate and effective vocabulary which suits the story (AF7)

Questions for guided reading

Starting off

NB: A Reading Running Record has been provided for this Task. You may wish to use it with children individually to assess AF1 prior to the guided reading session. Or you may wish to assess AF1 during the guided reading session.

Point out the setting (a Do It Yourself shop) before reading and ask the children if they have been to one. Ask them to describe what it was like.

Read and respond

Check that the children have understood the story using the following questions:
- **Why did Amy and her dad go to the Do It Yourself shop? (AF2)**
- What did Amy want to do in the shop? (AF2)
- **Why did Amy lose sight of Dad? (AF3)**
- **What did Amy ask the shop assistant to do? (AF2)**
- How do you know Dad was worried? (AF3)
- **What are the main events? Can you tell them in the order of the story? (AF2)**
- **What is wrong with these sentences?** *Soon Dad came wandering in. He looked very pale in the face.* Repeat with other sentences. (AF2)

Going deeper

Discuss any occasions when the children have thought they were lost – in a shop or elsewhere. What did they do and how did they feel? Encourage them to relate their own experience to the story characters.
- **How do you think Amy felt when she lost sight of Dad? (AF3)**
- How does the author help you to read with expression? (AF1)
- As well as Dad's spoken words, how else can you tell how he felt? (AF3)

Reflect

Discuss what Amy did when she lost sight of Dad. What would the children do if they were in the same situation? (AF6)

Task 1 Lost and Found!

Lost and Found!

"Amy," said Dad, "do you want to come to the Do It Yourself shop and get some gardening gloves?"

"Yes, please!" said Amy.

When they got there, Amy wanted to look at everything.

"Come on," said Dad. "We need to be quick."

Amy stopped to look at the tools. Then she lost sight of Dad.

"Dad!" she called, but there was no answer. He was nowhere to be seen!

She turned a corner, and there in front of her she saw the gardening gloves!

"At least I've found something," she thought.

She saw a shop assistant. "Please help," said Amy. "I've lost my dad."

The shop assistant took Amy to the office. Soon Dad came rushing in. He looked very red in the face.

"Oh, Amy," he said. "I've been so worried. I couldn't find you anywhere!"

"Look, Dad," she said. "I've found the gardening gloves!"

Task 1 Lost and Found!

Name: _____	Date: _____
Story: __Lost and Found!__	RW = 100

Story text to record child's reading	Strategies used
"Amy," said Dad, "do you want to come to the Do It Yourself shop and get some gardening gloves?" "Yes, please!" said Amy. When they got there, Amy wanted to look at everything. "Come on," said Dad. "We need to be quick." Amy stopped to look at the tools. Then she lost sight of Dad. "Dad!" she called, but there was no answer. He was nowhere to be seen! She turned a corner, and there in front of her she saw the gardening gloves! "At least I've found something," she thought. She saw a shop assistant. "Please help," said Amy.	
Miscues total:	

Reading Symbols

No errors	Miscues/errors
✓ = correct	T = told word
SC = self-corrected	O = omitted word
	^ = inserted word
	Write any incorrect word over target word.

Reading Strategies
Ph = phonic
G = graphic
S = syntactic
C = contextual

Find the number of miscues in the top row of this table to find the corresponding accuracy rate in the bottom row.

Miscue total	1	2	3	4	5	6	7	8	9	10	11	12	13	14	15
Accuracy rate	99%	98%	97%	96%	95%	94%	93%	92%	91%	90%	89%	88%	87%	86%	85%

95% or greater = comfortable level for independent reading. 94% or below = frustration level for independent reading.

Accuracy Rate = _____

The accuracy rate indicates how well the pupil uses a range of strategies, including accurate decoding of text, to read. Use the accuracy rate as evidence towards **AF1**.

Next steps: Refer to the 'Questions for guided reading' for *Lost and Found!* for comprehension questions in order to gather evidence about how well the pupil can read for meaning, including gathering other AF evidence, e.g. **AF2** and **AF3**.

Task 1 Lost and Found!

1. Why did Amy and her Dad go to the Do It Yourself shop?

....

....

....

2. Why did Amy lose sight of Dad?

....

....

....

3. How do you think Amy felt when she lost sight of Dad? Write in the thought bubble.

4. What did Amy ask the shop assistant to do?

....

....

Task 1 Lost and Found!

Task 1 Lost and Found!

5. What are the main events in the story? Write them down in the order they happen.

6. What is wrong with these sentences from the story? Cross out the wrong words. Write the correct words above them.

Soon Dad came wandering in. He looked very pale in the face.

"Oh, Amy," he shouted. "I've been so cross. I couldn't see you anywhere!"

"Look, Dad," she laughed. "I've lost the gardening gloves!"

Task 1 Lost and Found!

Main Assessment Focus: AF1 (use a range of strategies, including accurate decoding of text, to read for meaning)

Strategies used (NB: Use the Reading Running Record to provide assessment evidence for AF1)	Grid reference	Notes
Range of key words read on sight (e.g. lost, found, please, thought).	Level 2 / bullet 1	
Unfamiliar words decoded using appropriate strategies, e.g. blending sounds (e.g. gardening, corner, assistant).	Level 2 / bullet 2	
Some fluency of expression, e.g. taking account of punctuation, such as speech marks and exclamation marks.	Level 2 / bullet 3	
Range of strategies used mostly effectively to read with fluency, understanding and expression, e.g. taking account of speech marks and exclamation marks to show different characters and how they are feeling.	Level 3	

Main Assessment Focus: AF2 (understand, describe, select or retrieve information, events or ideas from texts and use quotation and reference to text)

Question	Exemplified responses	Grid reference	Notes
Why did Amy and her dad go to the Do It Yourself shop?	Straightforward information given, e.g. "to get some gardening gloves".	Level 2 / bullet 1	
	Straightforward information given though may mistakenly be elaborated on, e.g. "because her dad asked her to go".	Level 3 / bullet 1	
What are the main events? Can you tell them in the order of the story?	Characters and some main events are correct though some out of sequence.	Level 2 / bullet 1	
	Most points are sequenced correctly.	Level 3 / bullet 1	
What did Amy ask the shop assistant to do?	Straightforward information given, e.g. "to help".	Level 2 / bullet 1	
	As above, but with elaboration, e.g. "to help her because she had lost Dad".	Level 3 / bullet 2	
What is wrong with these sentences from the story?	Recognises which words are different from the sentences in the story by direct reference to the text.	Level 2 / bullet 1	
	Recognises that the meaning of the sentences has changed.	Level 3 / bullet 2	

Main Assessment Focus: AF3 (deduce, infer or interpret information, events or ideas from texts)

Question	Exemplified responses	Grid reference	Notes
Why did Amy lose sight of Dad?	Shows straightforward inference, e.g. "because she stopped to look at tools".	Level 2 / bullet 2	
	Response based on personal speculation, e.g. "She wasn't looking at him."	Level 3 / bullet 1	
How do you think Amy felt when she lost sight of Dad?	Expresses a simple plausible opinion, e.g. "scared".	Level 2 / bullet 1	
	Elaborates with reference to the text, e.g. "worried because she doesn't know where Dad is".	Level 3 / bullet 1	

Exemplified responses matched to levels of attainment are provided as a guide. As always, professional judgement must be used when assessing pupils' learning progression and a range of evidence should be gathered for each AF.

Task 1 Lost and Found!

Imagine you were lost in a shopping centre.

Choose an adjective (describing word) or phrase to make these sentences more interesting.

Then write one of your own in the box.

1. I got lost in the _____ shopping centre.

noisy   crowded   busy   vast   gleaming

> **My own different adjective**

2. I felt _____ .

scared   lonely   brave   angry   weepy

> **My own different adjective**

3. When I was found, I felt _____

_____ .

very happy   so relieved   safe again   a bit better

> **My own different phrase**

Task 1 Lost and Found!

4. Imagine you were lost in a shopping centre. What happened in the BEGINNING, MIDDLE and END of the story?

Think about:

- WHO was with you?

- WHERE in the shopping centre were you?

- WHAT happened?

Use the back of this sheet to make notes before writing your sentences.

BEGINNING

MIDDLE

END

Task 1 Lost and Found!

A pupil response within the range for Level 2 might be:

Questions 1–3 (AF7)

- Selects the most appropriate and obvious choices of vocabulary, e.g. the 'crowded' shopping centre; I felt 'scared'; I felt 'very happy'. Own adjectives and phrase are appropriate but generally unadventurous, e.g. 'big', 'giant'; 'afraid', 'frightened'; 'excited', 'joyful'.

Question 4 (AF1, AF4, AF5, AF6, AF7, AF8)

AF1

Relevant ideas (e.g. 'We went to the shoping hool [hall]'; 'when I tund round and my dad was not there!').
Some repetitive phrases ('I went', 'we went', 'then we went'). Then varies the verb ('we came to').
Shows and maintains viewpoint: 'I felt really terafid'; 'his hceeks were red'; 'I was very pleased'.

AF6

Grammatically correct.
Use of full stops showing some accurate sentence demarcation though omitted occasionally. One use of exclamation mark ('my dad was not there!').

AF7

Simple, speech-like vocabulary conveys relevant meaning ('I went to a shoping center'; 'I looked at some toys').
Some adventurous word choices ('terafid', 'came rushing in').

AF4

Sections unclear with no use of paragraphing or line breaks.

AF5

Some variation in sentence openings: 'A hor later'; 'When he found me'.
Consistent use of past tense.

AF8

Most high frequency words correctly spelled.
Errors in words with inflected endings ('shoping', 'finaly').
Phonetic attempts at spelling ('hool', 'terafid', 'resepshon').

I went to a shoping center with my dad. we went to the shoping hool then we went into a shoping hool agttin finally we came to a shop I looked at some toys when I tund round and my dad was not there! I felt reay terafid. I went to resepshon. A hore later my dad come rushing in where have you been he said. his hceeks were red. when he found me I was very pleased

Task 1 Lost and Found!

A pupil response within the range for Level 3 might be:

Questions 1–3 (AF7)

- Makes more interesting vocabulary choices, e.g. the 'gleaming' shopping centre; I felt 'lonely'; I felt 'so relieved'. Own words and phrase show a wider vocabulary and more adventurous choices, e.g. 'bustling', 'enormous'; 'terrified'; 'worried'; 'overjoyed', 'thankful'.

Question 4 (AF1, AF4, AF5, AF6, AF7, AF8)

AF1

Appropriate ideas and content included. Elaboration of ideas ('ten minutes time', 'got bord of looking', 'I dreamed about what had happened'). Some expression of viewpoint ('It was worse and frightening').

AF6

Mostly accurate use of full stops and capital letters to demarcate sentences. Use of speech punctuation not always accurate. (e.g. "Yes please I said; "Mum, Mum," Mum.) Use of commas limited to repetitions (e.g. 'Mum, Mum, Mum'; 'Tasha, Tasha').

AF7

Simple vocabulary appropriate to task.
Some adventurous word choices: 'relieved', 'bored', 'frightening'.

AF4

Ideas organised into paragraphs but abrupt movement between paragraphs.
Evidence of links between sentences within paragraphs ('carried on looking at clothes. After a while...').

AF5

Variation in sentence openings.
Mostly simple and compound sentences joined by 'and'.
Some variation of tenses, e.g. 'Shall we go home now?'

AF8

Correct spelling of the majority of words.
Some phonetic attempts (e.g. 'bord', 'herd', 'oky').

One Summers day Mum said to me "would you like to go to a running shop" "yes please I said When we were there we went into a running shop. I go

I got bord of looking at the running shop clothes so I went into a different shop. In ten minutes time Mum didnt know were I was and she started to call for me = Tasha, Tasha. First I forgot about Mum and carried on looking at the clothes After a while I did get worried and I started to call for Mum "Mum, Mum," Mum. Mum herd me and came rushing in and I was so relived. Mum said to me "dont go off like that again unless you tell me oky" "yes mum.

"Shall we go home now" "Tasha" "Yes please When we got home I told Dad what had happened and he said " you shouldnt go off like that again " "Yes Dad I said. Next it was bedtime and I went to sleep. I dreamed about what had happened. It was worse and frightening!

Task 1 Lost and Found!

Reading

Next steps for developing AF1

Children will need different support depending on the type of miscues they make. For support with phonic skills (e.g. blending, etc), refer to the guidance in *Letters and Sounds* (DCSF ref: 00281-2007).

In addition, ensure that children play games such as Sound Snap, Match the Pairs and Bingo. By asking appropriate questions, such as the following, during shared and guided reading, children can be encouraged to read for meaning and use a range of strategies:

- Would ... fit there?
- Does that make sense?
- Do you think it looks like ...?
- Check it. Does it look right and sound right?

This activity should be part of a range of evidence gathered for AF1. Evidence for AF1 can be gathered from a range of sources, such as:

- observations during guided and shared reading;
- observations during phonic activities;
- other reading running records or teacher records;
- Home/School records.

Task 3 on pages 30 to 41 is another opportunity to gather evidence for AF1 using a running record.

Next steps for developing AF2

Children will benefit from further practice in answering literal, fact-based questions. Useful questions you could ask when reading a piece of text together might be:

- What happened in the beginning / middle / end of the story?
- What did [character x] do?
- Where did the story take place?

This activity should be part of a range of evidence gathered for AF2, from a range of sources, such as:

- observations during guided and shared reading;
- drama activities such as hot-seating;
- book reviews.

Tasks 3–6 on pages 30 to 72 provide other opportunities to gather evidence for AF2.

Next steps for developing AF3

Children will benefit from further practice in answering inferential questions and using reference to the text to support answers. Useful questions you could ask when reading a piece of text together might be:

- Why do you think x felt the way they did? What in the story makes you think that?
- Why did x do that? What lines suggest that?
- What was the most exciting part? Why do you think that?

This activity should be part of a range of evidence gathered for AF3 from a range of sources, such as:

- observations during guided and shared reading;
- creating character profiles or thought bubbles;
- speaking and listening and drama activities, such as role-play and hot-seating.

Task 4 on pages 42 to 51 and Task 5 on pages 52 to 62 provide other opportunities to gather evidence for AF3.

Task 1 Lost and Found!

Writing

Next steps for developing AF1

In order to progress children's ability to write interesting, imaginative and thoughtful stories with a clear opening, middle and ending, give them opportunities to:

- retell stories orally and through drama activities;
- play vocabulary games (e.g. from *Grammar for Writing* DCSF ref: 0107-2000, such as creating human sentences or phrases, adding, substituting or extending them for different effects: funny, silly, dramatic etc; 'meaning' snap or pelmanism) in order to help them develop a wider vocabulary and use more apt and adventurous word choices;
- choose subject matter that interests them.

This activity should be part of a range of evidence gathered for AF1, such as Task 2 on pages 21 to 29 and Task 3 on pages 30 to 41.

Next steps for developing AF6

Provide the children with opportunities to develop their understanding of syntax and punctuation in shared and guided writing sessions by, for example:

- thinking aloud how to use punctuation to support meaning and create effects, e.g. 'Now I want to ask a question, to hook the reader in. *What was it?* I need to use a question mark to make the reader aware that it is a question.'
- identifying sentences from the child's writing to be improved. Talk about how punctuation could be added or changed, and amend them verbally and in writing.

This activity should be part of a range of evidence gathered for AF6, such as Tasks 4 and 5 on pages 42 to 62.

Next steps for developing AF7

Provide further practice in selecting and using a range of descriptive vocabulary for impact and effect by, for example:

- writing short setting and character descriptions;
- editing and improving their own and others' writing;
- using class and individual word banks.

This activity should be part of a range of evidence gathered for AF7. All the Tasks in this book may provide such evidence.

Task 2 On my way from school

Aims of this task

This task is designed to help you make judgements about children's performance in Reading **AF5** and **AF6** (with opportunities to assess AF1 and AF4 as well) and Writing **AF1, AF2, AF3** and **AF7** (with opportunity to assess AF6 as well). Children read and respond to a short poem 'On my way from school'. They then write a cumulative poem of their own.

Related Renewed Framework unit

Poetry Unit 1: Patterns on the page

Renewed Framework objectives

7.1, 7.2, 7.5, 8.3, 9.1, 9.4

Key concepts

Reading
- identify and comment on the structure of the poem (AF4)
- identify adjectives and their purpose and effect in the poem (AF5)
- understand the poet's purpose (AF6)

Writing
- use imagination in writing the ending of a poem (AF1)
- think about the effect on the reader (AF2)
- write a poem using a patterned-language structure(AF3)
- build up the effect through careful language choices (AF7)

Questions for guided reading

Starting off

Before the children read the poem, read them the title and the first line. What do they think the poem is going to be about? Can they tell whether the poem will be funny or serious? What do *they* do on their way home from school? Then read the poem. (AF1)

Read and respond

Check that the children have understood the poem, using the following questions:

- **Look at sentences 3 to 7 of the poem. How is each one different from the one before it? (AF4)**
- **What adjectives are used to describe the cat? (AF5)**
- **Which adjectives tell us what the cat looked like? Which tell us what sort of cat he was? (AF5)**

Going deeper

- **Read the first 7 sentences. What does the poet want you to think about the cat? (AF6)**
- **Read sentence 8. What does the child in the poem feel about the cat? Which words make you think that? (AF6)**
- Why do you think the poet gave the name 'Cuddles' to the cat? (AF3, AF6)
- How does the last line make you feel about the whole poem? (AF6)

Reflect

Invite the children to read the poem aloud and discuss how best to read the poem as a group. Do they know any other poems that use a similar cumulative language pattern? (AF4)

Task 2 On my way from school

On my way from school

On my way from school I saw a cat.

It was a fat cat.

It was a black, fat cat.

It was a big, black, fat cat.

It was a hairy, big, black, fat cat.

It was a scary, hairy, big, black, fat cat.

It was a mean, scary, hairy, big, black, fat cat.

It was my mean, scary, hairy, big, black, fat cat called Cuddles,

and she followed me home.

Roger Stevens

Task 2 On my way from school

1. Look at sentences 3 to 7 of the poem. How is each one different from the one before it?

2. What adjectives are used to describe the cat? Write them in the boxes.

3a. Underline the adjectives that tell us what the cat looked like.

3b. What do the other adjectives tell us about the cat?

4. Read the first 7 sentences. What does the poet want you to think about the cat?

5a. Read sentence 8. What does the child in the poem feel about the cat?

5b. Underline the words that make you think that.

Task 2 On my way from school

Main Assessment Focus: AF5 (explain and comment on writers' use of language, including grammatical and literary features at word and sentence level)

Question	Exemplified responses	Grid reference	Notes
What adjectives are used to describe the cat?	With support, able to understand the term 'adjective', able to identify most 'describing' words.	Level 2 / bullet 1	
	Without support, able to identify all adjectives.	Level 3 / bullet 1	
Which adjectives tell us what the cat looked like? Which tell us what sort of cat he was?	Identifies some appropriate adjectives about appearance, but usually won't distinguish between appearance and character descriptions.	Level 2 / bullet 2	
	Identifies 'scary' and 'mean' without prompting and may make an unsolicited comment about the change of adjectives that describe appearance to those relating to character, e.g. "It says first what the cat looks like, then what he is like."	Level 3	

Main Assessment Focus: AF6 (identify and comment on writers' purposes and viewpoints and the overall effect of the text on the reader)

Question	Exemplified responses	Grid reference	Notes
Read the first 7 sentences. What does the poet want you to think about the cat?	Shows basic awareness of purpose, e.g. "He wants you to think the cat is mean and scary."	Level 2 / bullet 1	
	Shows awareness of purpose and attempts some interpretation, e.g. "He uses mean and scary to make you think the child is frightened by the cat."	Level 3 / bullet 1	
Read sentence 8. What does the child in the poem feel about the cat? Which words make you think that?	Shows simple inference, e.g. "The child isn't scared because it is his cat. It says my."	Level 2 / bullet 2	
	May suggest that the child is proud or fond of the cat, e.g. "He isn't scared. He says my like he's proud to have the cat and the cat is called Cuddles which is a nice, not a scary name."	Level 3 / bullet 2	

Other Assessment Focus: AF4 (identify and comment on the structure and organisation of texts, including grammatical and presentational features at text level)

Question	Exemplified responses	Grid reference	Notes
Look at sentences 3 to 7 of the poem. How is each one different from the one before it?	Identifies that there is a structural difference, but no comment, e.g. "They are longer each time."	Level 2	
	As above, but able to elaborate, e.g. "Each sentence is longer because the poet adds another word to describe the cat."	Level 3	

Exemplified responses matched to levels of attainment are provided as a guide. As always, professional judgement must be used when assessing pupils' learning progression and a range of evidence should be gathered for each AF.

Task 2 On my way from school

Write your own poem about an animal you see on the way from school.

1. Plan it first.

   a. What animal will your poem be about? Write it in the centre box.

   b. Write some adjectives (describing words) to describe your animal.

2. Now write your poem.

   REMEMBER! Add a new adjective to each line. Write your own ending for your poem.

   On my way from school I saw a

   It was a

   It was a

   It was a

   It was a

   It was a

   It was a

Task 2 On my way from school

A pupil response within the range for Level 2 might be:

Question 1a (AF1, AF2)

- Choice of animal is relevant and appropriate to the task, following the model of the stimulus text, e.g. bird, dog, rabbit or some other familiar pet.

Question 1b (AF1, AF7)

- Apt and some adventurous adjective choices appropriate for the subject, e.g. bird: 'black', 'flying', 'scary'; dog: 'big', 'brown', 'barking'; rabbit: 'little', 'fluffy', 'hopping'.

Question 2 (AF1, AF2, AF3, AF6, AF7)

AF1
Relevant ideas (the choice of animal) and appropriate adjectives chosen for the task.

AF2
Appropriate ideas, content and style based on the model poem.

AF3
Sequenced correctly. Clear opening and closing adopted from the model poem.

AF7
Some adventurous vocabulary, e.g. 'heree' (hairy), 'bran' (brown), 'meen' (mean).

AF6
Consistent use of full stops to end each line. Some use of commas in the list of adjectives, but inconsistent.

On my way from school I saw a dog.

It was a big dog.

It was a fat, big dog.

It was a meen, fat, big dog.

It was a bran, meen, fat, big dog.

It was a heree, bran, meen, fat, big dog.

It was a screy, heree, bran, meen, fat, big dog, called Alix.

Task 2 On my way from school

A pupil response within the range for Level 3 might be:

Question 1a (AF1, AF2)

- Choice of animal shows a greater degree of imagination and humour, e.g. a fantasy creature, such as a dragon or a creature that is not usually considered a pet, such as an elephant, a snail, a panda.

Question 1b (AF1, AF7)

- Chooses adjectives thoughtfully so that they are mostly relevant to chosen animal. Shows some attempt to use adjectives for effect, e.g. snail: 'slimy', 'gooey'; dog: 'floppy-eared', 'pink-nosed'.

Question 2 (AF1, AF2, AF3, AF6, AF7)

AF1
Appropriate content for the task with imaginative choice of subject (snail).
Evidence of viewpoint in the imaginative ending.

AF2
Appropriate ideas, content and style adopted from the model poem.
Ending shows attention to the effect on the reader.

AF3
Clearly sequenced, with opening adopted from the model poem, and a clearly signalled ending. Shows imagination and humour in varying the ending: '… and that is why…'.

On my way from school I saw a _snail._

It was a _slimy snail._

It was a _gooey, slimy, snail._

It was a _ugly, gooey, slimy snail._

It was a _fat, ugly, gooey, slimy snail._

It was a _plant eating, fat, gooey, slimy snail._

It was a _crunching, plant eating, fat, gooey, slimy snail._

I got stuck in its tracks and that is why I'm late for tea.

AF7
Appropriate vocabulary, with some well-chosen words for effect ('goey' (gooey), 'slimy').

AF6
Consistent use of full stops to end each line. Consistent use of commas in the list of adjectives.

Task 2 On my way from school

Reading

Next steps for developing AF5

Children will benefit from further practice in analysing text at sentence and word level. Identifying examples of language features and articulating the effect will help to progress their understanding of why a writer chooses words and phrases in poetry. Questions you could ask to stimulate further thought include:

- What does x make you see in your mind's eye?
- What other ways are there to say this?
- How does x make you feel?

This activity should be part of a range of evidence gathered for AF5. Evidence for AF5 can be gathered from a range of sources, such as:

- observations during guided and shared reading;
- activities such as text marking or annotating;
- listening and responding to poems, rhymes, advertising jingles etc.

Task 4 on pages 42 to 51 is another opportunity to gather evidence for AF5.

Next steps for developing AF6

Children will benefit from further practice in expressing personal opinions and preferences, and developing a growing awareness of the purpose and viewpoint of the writer. Questions you could ask to stimulate thought include:

- What do you think about … ?
- How does this story / poem make you feel?
- How does the writer / poet feel? How do you know?
- Who is telling the story / speaking in the poem?

This activity should be part of a range of evidence gathered for AF6. Evidence for AF6 can be gathered from a range of sources, such as:

- book reviews;
- drama and role-play activities;
- discussion of visual texts.

Task 6 on pages 63 to 72 is another opportunity to gather evidence for AF6.

Writing

Next steps for developing AF1

In order to progress children's ability to write imaginative texts, for example poems that use patterned language, give them opportunities to:

- participate in oral poetry-making activities and oral performances;
- in shared reading, read poems that use repeated and patterned language and use them as models, adding to and innovating on them;
- find and use new and interesting words and phrases;
- orally rehearse their idea;
- take risks with their choices of language.

This activity should be part of a range of evidence gathered for AF1, such as Task 1 on pages 9 to 20 and Task 3 on pages 30 to 41.

Task 2 On my way from school

Writing (continued)

Next steps for developing AF2

In order to progress children's ability to write appropriately for the task and with reader and purpose in mind, encourage them to:

- think of a specific reader for their writing;
- think in advance about what they want that reader to think and feel;
- in shared and guided writing activities, work on simple poems to demonstrate the way poems are formed (structure, etc);
- orally rehearse their ideas;
- use simple pattern structures to support their writing.

This activity should be part of a range of evidence gathered for AF2, such as Task 3 on pages 30 to 41 and Task 5 on pages 52 to 62.

Next steps for developing AF3

In order to progress children's ability to organise and write whole texts (poems as well as stories and non-fiction), encourage them to:

- use planning techniques such as graphic organisers, story boards etc which will benefit them by helping them structure their ideas to ensure they draw their writing to an appropriate conclusion;
- experiment in re-ordering sections of the story / poem they have written;
- in shared and guided reading sessions, explore how writers link and sequence events and ideas.

This activity should be part of a range of evidence gathered for AF3, such as Task 3 on pages 30 to 41 and Task 6 on pages 63 to 72.

Next steps for developing AF7

Provide further practice in selecting and using a range of descriptive vocabulary for impact and effect by, for example:

- providing word and sentence activities that involve replacing words in sentences, extending sentences, re-writing sentences in the style of … and so on;
- writing short setting and character descriptions;
- using class and individual word banks;
- editing and improving their own and others' writing.

This activity should be part of a range of evidence gathered for AF7. All the Tasks in this book may provide such evidence.

Task 3 Mother Holle

Aims of this task

This task is designed to help you make judgements about children's performance in Reading **AF1**, **AF2** and **AF7** (with opportunity to assess AF3 as well), and Writing **AF1**, **AF2**, **AF3** and **AF7** (with opportunities to assess AF4 and AF6 as well). Children read and respond to an extract from the beginning of 'Mother Holle', a traditional story. They identify time-related words and phrases that indicate basic sequencing and write their own ending for the story.

Related Renewed Framework unit

Narrative Unit 2: Traditional stories

Renewed Framework objectives

5.1, 7.2, 8.2, 9.1, 9.4, 10.2

Key concepts

Reading
- read fluently with understanding and expression (AF1)
- identify and order key events in the story (AF2)
- deduce, infer ideas from texts (AF3)
- relate features of the story to other traditional tales (AF7)

Writing
- use imagination to write a story ending (AF1)
- sequence events in a story using connecting words and phrases (AF3)
- use interesting and lively vocabulary (AF7)

Questions for guided reading

Starting off

NB: A Reading Running Record has been provided for this Task. You may wish to use it with children individually to assess AF1 prior to the guided reading session. Or you may wish to assess AF1 during the guided reading session.

Explain that this text is the beginning of a retelling of a traditional story called 'Mother Holle'. Point out any new or unusual vocabulary (such as 'idle' and 'spindle') and discuss the meanings before asking the children to read.

Read and respond

Check that the children have understood the story, using the following questions:
- **What are the main events of the story? Can you tell them in order? (AF2)**
- **Why did Rosa jump into the well? (AF2)**
- How are Rosa and Kate different? (AF2)
- How did Rosa make it snow on Earth? (AF2)

Going deeper

- **Which words or phrases in the story can you recognise from other stories you have read? (AF7)**
- **Which characters can you recognise from other stories you have read? (AF7)**
- **What do you think Rosa thought when Mother Holle invited her to stay? (AF3)**

Reflect

Invite the children to speculate about how the story might continue and what might happen at the end. (AF3)

Task 3 Mother Holle

Mother Holle

Once upon a time there was a girl called Rosa, who lived with her kindly father, her cruel stepmother and her lazy and spoiled stepsister, Kate.

The stepmother gave Kate the best food and the best clothes even though she was idle all day long. Poor Rosa ate leftovers, wore rags and did all the housework. When Rosa finished the housework, her stepmother sent her out to spin by the well.

One day, Rosa was working so hard at spinning that her fingers began to bleed. As she bent over the well to wash the blood from the spindle, it slipped from her hand and fell in.

Rosa's cruel stepmother ordered her to get the spindle back.

So Rosa went to the well and jumped in. She awoke in a beautiful meadow.

Task 3 Mother Holle

Before long, Rosa came to a little house. A strange old woman came out.

"Don't be afraid, child," said the old woman kindly. "I am Mother Holle. Come and stay with me and help with my housework."

She spoke so kindly that Rosa said she would stay.

"Very good," said Mother Holle. "But remember, when you make my bed you must shake it up until the feathers fly about, so that then it will snow on Earth."

So Rosa lived with Mother Holle, where she worked hard and was looked after well.

Whenever she made the bed, she shook it up until the feathers flew about, and snow fell on Earth.

Name: _____	Date: _____
Story: Mother Holle	RW = 100

Story text to record child's reading	Strategies used
Once upon a time there was a girl called Rosa, who lived with her kindly father, her cruel stepmother and her lazy and spoiled stepsister, Kate. The stepmother gave Kate the best food and the best clothes even though she was idle all day long. Poor Rosa ate leftovers, wore rags and did all the housework. When Rosa finished the housework, her stepmother sent her out to spin by the well. One day, Rosa was working so hard at spinning that her fingers began to bleed. As she bent over the well to wash the blood from the spindle, it [slipped from her hand and fell in.]	

Miscues total:

Reading Symbols

No errors	Miscues/errors
✓ = correct	T = told word
SC = self-corrected	O = omitted word
	^ = inserted word
	Write any incorrect word over target word.

Reading Strategies
Ph = phonic
G = graphic
S = syntactic
C = contextual

Find the number of miscues in the top row of this table to find the corresponding accuracy rate in the bottom row.

Miscue total	1	2	3	4	5	6	7	8	9	10	11	12	13	14	15
Accuracy rate	99%	98%	97%	96%	95%	94%	93%	92%	91%	90%	89%	88%	87%	86%	85%

95% or greater = comfortable level for independent reading. 94% or below = frustration level for independent reading.

Accuracy Rate = _____

The accuracy rate indicates how well the pupil uses a range of strategies, including accurate decoding of text, to read. Use the accuracy rate as evidence towards **AF1**.

Next steps: Refer to the 'Questions for guided reading' for *Mother Holle* for comprehension questions in order to gather evidence about how well the pupil can read for meaning, including gathering other AF evidence, e.g. **AF2**, **AF3** and **AF7**.

Task 3 Mother Holle

1. What are the main events of the story? Can you tell them in order?

1. ....

   ....

2. ....

   ....

3. ....

   ....

4. ....

   ....

2a. Why did Rosa jump into the well? Underline the answer you think is the best one.

a) Because she had dropped the spindle into it.

b) Because her stepmother told her to get the spindle back.

c) Because she had made her fingers bleed.

d) Because she wanted to get away from her stepmother.

2b. Why do you think your answer is best?

Task 3 Mother Holle

3. Which words or phrases in the story can you recognise from other stories you have read? Write them.

4. Which characters can you recognise from other stories you have read? Write them in the space below.

Rosa, a hard-working girl

A cruel stepmother

A spoiled and lazy stepsister

A kindly old woman

5. What do you think Rosa thought when Mother Holle invited her to stay?

Task 3 Mother Holle

Main Assessment Focus: AF1 (use a range of strategies, including accurate decoding of text, to read for meaning)

Strategies used (NB: Use the **Reading Running Record** to provide assessment evidence for AF1)	Grid reference	Notes
• Range of key words read on sight (e.g. Once, spoiled, stepmother, fingers).	Level 2 / bullet 1	
• Unfamiliar words decoded using appropriate strategies, e.g. blending sounds (e.g. cruel, idle, spindle).	Level 2 / bullet 2	
• Some fluency of expression, e.g. taking account of punctuation, such as commas.	Level 2 / bullet 3	
• Range of strategies used mostly effectively to read with fluency, understanding and expression, e.g. taking account of punctuation for pace and traditional story language for tone and expression.	Level 3	

Main Assessment Focus: AF2 (understand, describe, select or retrieve information, events or ideas from texts and use quotation and reference to text)

Question	Exemplified responses	Grid reference	Notes
What are the main events of the story? Can you tell them in order?	Retells main events with prompting, but may include more than necessary.	Level 2 / bullet 1	
	Recalls and sequences main points correctly, e.g. Rosa was spinning so hard her fingers bled; She dropped the spindle into the well and jumped in to get it; She landed in a meadow where she went to live with Mother Holle; Rosa shook Mother Holle's bed to make it snow on Earth.	Level 3 / bullet 2	
Why did Rosa jump into the well?	Selects answer a) as being the most obvious.	Level 2 / bullet 2	
	Selects answer b) with justification, e.g. she probably wouldn't have bothered to get it back if her stepmother hadn't told her to.	Level 3 / bullet 2	

Main Assessment Focus: AF7 (relate texts to their social, cultural and historical traditions)

Which characters can you recognise from other stories you have read?	Recognises some of the characters (e.g. stepmother and lazy stepsister) and associates them with one well-known story (e.g. Cinderella).	Level 2 / bullet 1	
	Recognises most of the stereotypical fairy story characters and associates some with more than one well-known story, though may be unable to associate Mother Holle.	Level 3 / bullet 1	
Which words or phrases can you recognise from other stories you have read?	Recognises some story-book language, e.g. Once upon a time; one day.	Level 2 / bullet 1	
	Recognises story book language and some typical fairytale vocabulary, e.g. cruel stepmother (Cinderella); worked so hard at spinning (Rumpelstiltskin).	Level 3 / bullet 1	

Other Assessment Focus: AF3 (relate texts to their cultural and historical contexts)

What do you think Rosa thought when Mother Holle invited her to stay?	Simple, plausible inference, using evidence from the story, e.g. "I will stay because this woman seems kind."	Level 2 / bullet 1	
	Extended inference, e.g. "I will stay because this woman is kind and not cruel like my stepmother."	Level 3 / bullet 1	

Exemplified responses matched to levels of attainment are provided as a guide. As always, professional judgement must be used when assessing pupils' learning progression and a range of evidence should be gathered for each AF.

Task 3 Mother Holle

1. Here is what happened next in the story, but the sentences are in the wrong order. Write a number next to each sentence to show the right order.

After a while, Mother Holle saw that Kate was lazy and didn't bother to shake up the bed. ☐

One day, Rosa became homesick. ☐

So Mother Holle covered Rosa in gold as a reward and sent her home. ☐

In the end, Mother Holle covered Kate in tar as a punishment and sent her home. ☐

When Rosa's stepmother saw Rosa covered in gold, she sent Kate down the well to Mother Holle's house. ☐

2. Which story words and phrases helped you to put the sentences in the right order? Make a list.

1. ....

2. ....

3. ....

4. ....

5. ....

3. What do you think happened when the stepmother saw Kate covered in tar? Write your own ending. Use a separate piece of paper.

REMEMBER! Use some good connecting words to link your ideas and sentences.

Task 3 Mother Holle

A pupil response within the range for Level 2 might be:

Question 1 (AF3)
- With support, shows some ability to sequence sentences to create a story (e.g. using 'One day' and 'In the end' as markers for beginning and end), though sequence may not always be accurate.

Question 2 (AF3)
- Shows some understanding of how time-related words and phrases signal sequence by identifying some of the more obvious time-related words and phrases, e.g. 'So', 'In the end'.

Question 3 (AF1, AF2, AF3, AF4, AF6, AF7)

AF1

Mostly relevant ideas, e.g. 'Rosea why did you cover Kate in tar said Rosa's stepmother.' 'Shes the person who lives in the well ...' 'All show you ...'.
Some apt word choices showing the setting, e.g. 'meddo', 'entered the house'.

AF2

Some attempt to adopt the appropriate style, e.g. the stepmother's attitude shown by accusing Rosa ('Rosea why did you cover Kate in tar said Rosa's stepmother' and 'Sow said the stepmother where is this womon').

AF3

Basic sequencing of ideas.
Time-related words to sequence events: 'So the next day', 'Soon', 'A little later', 'Sudenly'.
No opening or closing signalled to readers.

AF7

Simple, speech-like vocabulary that is appropriate to the form, e.g. 'So they did apeea in a medo rite in front of her house.'

AF4

Lacking in paragraphs or sections.

AF6

Most sentences demarcated by capital letters and full stops. No use of speech punctuation or question marks. However, use of possessive apostrophe: 'Rosa's'.

> RoSea why did you cover kate in tar Said Rosa's stepmother. It woseent me said Rosa. it was mother hole hoos whoos mother hole said the step-mother. Shes the person who lives in the well said Rosa. All Show you said Rosa. Sow the next day Rosa snowed her Stepmother mother holes. Soon they reeched the well. Jump down the well and yourl apeea in a meddo rite infront of her house said Rosa. Sow they did apeea in a medo rite in front of her house. A little t-later they entered the house. but there wsost nowone inside Sudenly they heard the toilet flush. Sow said the stepmother where is this womon.

Task 3 Mother Holle

A pupil response within the range for Level 3 might be:

Question 1 (AF3)
- Sentences mostly sequenced logically and correctly; demonstrating awareness of how the events relate to one another, e.g. the stepmother seeing Rosa covered in gold comes after Mother Holle covering Rosa in gold.

Question 2 (AF3)
- Identifies most of the appropriate time-related words and phrases as indicators of sequence (e.g. 'One day', 'After a while', 'So', 'In the end'), but may not identify 'When' (at the beginning of adverbial clause) as one.

Question 3 (AF1, AF2, AF3, AF4, AF6, AF7)

AF1

Shows some attempt to engage the reader, e.g. description of characters' feelings; and imagination in ending the story – 'Kate and the stepmother fell down a deep deep hole'.

AF2

Evidence of viewpoint expressed ('fyureaus', 'you are spost to be covered in gold', 'Rosa started to lafe'). Detail included in an attempt to engage the reader, e.g. 'When they got in the garden the well was vanished'; 'fell down a deep deep hole'.

When stepmother saw Kate covered in tar she was fyureaus why was not Rosa covered in tar insted said the stepmother you are spost to be covered in gold. Rosa started to lafe it's not funny funny said Kate and her stepmother STOP!!!! soted the stepmother where did you get covered in tar come with me. When they got in the garden the well was vanished SUDUNLY Kate and stepmother fell down a deep deep hole the well was back in it's place Rosa Rosa jumped back in the well then it vanished agina Rosa went to Mother holle cotage and never went back to that hose again

AF3

Opening and closing clearly signalled.
Ideas are clearly sequenced and drawn to a conclusion.
Time-related vocabulary: 'When', 'Sudunly'.

AF7

Simple, speech-like vocabulary. Some words chosen for effect: 'fyureaus', 'vanished', 'SUDUNLY'.

AF4

Lacking in paragraphs or sections.
Some linking of ideas in the beginning, but not maintained.

AF6

Use of capital letters and some full stops, but not consistent. Use of apostrophe for contraction (it's) and exclamation marks.

Task 3 Mother Holle

Reading

Next steps for developing AF1

Children will need different support depending on the type of miscues they make. For support with phonic skills (e.g. blending, etc), refer to the guidance in *Letters and Sounds* (DCSF ref: 00281-2007). In addition, ensure that children play games such as Sound Snap, Match the Pairs and Bingo. By asking appropriate questions, such as the following, during shared and guided reading, children can be encouraged to read for meaning and use a range of strategies:

- Would ... fit there?
- Does that make sense?
- Do you think it looks like ...?
- Check it. Does it look right and sound right?

This activity should be part of a range of evidence gathered for AF1. Evidence for AF1 can be gathered from a range of sources, such as:

- observations during guided and shared reading;
- observations during phonic activities;
- other reading running records or teacher records;
- Home/School records.

Task 1 on pages 9 to 20 is another opportunity to gather evidence for AF1 using a running record.

Next steps for developing AF2

Children will benefit from further practice in answering literal, fact-based questions. Useful questions you could ask when reading a piece of text together might be:

- List the main events that take place in this story.
- What happened after x? What happened before y?
- What did [x character] do?
- Where did the story take place?

This activity should be part of a range of evidence gathered for AF2. Evidence for AF2 can be gathered from a range of sources, such as:

- observations during guided and shared reading;
- drama activities, such as recreating a story;
- book reviews;
- finding information from other sources such as illustrations, maps, diagrams.

Task 1 on pages 9 to 20 and Tasks 4–6 on pages 42–72 provide other opportunities to gather evidence for AF2.

Next steps for developing AF7

Children will benefit from further practice in relating texts to their social, cultural and historical contexts and literary traditions by exploring language use and comparing how texts are the same or different from one another. Questions you could ask to stimulate thought include:

- How is story x similar to story y?
- In what place is the story set? In what time?
- Why does the story use this sort of language / opening sentence?

This activity should be part of a range of evidence gathered for AF7. Evidence for AF7 can be gathered from a range of sources, such as:

- observations during guided and shared reading;
- children's writing and contributions to shared and guided writing.

Task 3 Mother Holle

Writing

Next steps for developing AF1

In order to progress children's ability to write imaginative, interesting and thoughtful stories – and in particular, traditional stories – provide them with a wide variety of traditional stories in shared and guided reading and writing to use as models.

In addition, alternative versions of well-known traditional stories can be a rich source of ideas and demonstrate how other writers have used the language and style of traditional stories and innovated on the plot.

This activity should be part of a range of evidence gathered for AF1, such as Tasks 1 and 2 on pages 9 to 29.

Next steps for developing AF2

In order to progress children's ability to write appropriately for the task and with reader and purpose in mind, encourage them to:
• think of a specific reader for their writing;
• think in advance about what they want that reader to think and feel;
• in shared and guided writing activities, discuss and list features that are appropriate to the form;
• orally rehearse their ideas;
• use simple pattern structures to support their writing.

This activity should be part of a range of evidence gathered for AF2, such as Task 2 on pages 21 to 29 and Task 5 on pages 52 to 62.

Next steps for developing AF3

Provide further practice sequencing and linking ideas and events, for example, by:
• finding examples of words or phrases in fiction and non-fiction that link sentences;
• in shared and guided reading sessions, exploring how writers link and sequence events and ideas;
• editing and improving own and others' writing;
• experimenting in re-ordering sections of a story they have written.

This activity should be part of a range of evidence gathered for AF3, such as Task 2 on pages 21 and 29 and Task 6 on pages 63 to 72.

Next steps for developing AF7

Provide further practice in selecting and using an appropriate style and vocabulary by, for example:
• providing word and sentence activities that involve replacing words in sentences, extending sentences, re-writing sentences in the style of … and so on;
• giving opportunities to continue a range of different stories from different genres;
• changing a story's beginning, middle or ending while retaining the style and tone of the story;
• writing new episodes for familiar stories.

This activity should be part of a range of evidence gathered for AF7. All the tasks in this book provide opportunities to gather such evidence.

Task 4 Electrical Circuits

Aims of this task

This task is designed to help you make judgements about children's performance in Reading **AF2**, **AF3**, **AF4** and **AF5** (with opportujity to assess AF1 as well) and Writing **AF5**, **AF6** and **AF7** (with opportunities to assess AF3 and AF8 as well). Children read and respond to a short explanation text about how an electrical circuit works. They then write an explanation of their own.

Related Renewed Framework unit

Non-fiction Unit 2: Explanations

Renewed Framework objectives

5.2, 7.1, 7.3, 9.1, 9.3, 9.5, 11.1

Key concepts

Reading

- find specific information by referring to the text (AF2)
- deduce what occurs when the circuit is broken (AF3)
- understand the purpose of features in the text (AF4)
- identify and understand subject-specific vocabulary (AF5)

Writing

- write clear sentences for an explanation (AF5)
- use simple punctuation in sentences accurately (AF6)
- use technical vocabulary (AF7)

Questions for guided reading

Starting off

Before reading, explain to the children that they are going to read an explanation of how an electrical circuit works. Discuss what they already know about electricity. What things use electricity to work? Which things do you have to plug in and which work with batteries? Can you think of words that relate to electricity? Discuss subject-specific words such as *electricity*, *circuit*, *battery*, *bulb* and *wires*, and ensure that the children know their meanings before asking them to read. (AF5) Read the text. (AF1)

Read and respond

Check the children's understanding of the text, using the following questions:

- **What is an electrical circuit? (AF2)**
- **After the introduction, where should you start to read? How do you know? (AF4)**
- **Why do batteries have a + and – sign on them? (AF2)**
- What other meaning do you know for the word 'bulb'? (AF5)

Going deeper

- Find the words in bold print. Why do you think they are written in bold? (AF4)
- **How does the diagram help to explain how a circuit works? (AF4)**
- Why does the text use present tense verbs? (AF4)
- **Why does the writer use the word 'flows' to describe the movement of electricity?(AF5)**
- **What do you think would happen if a wire in the circuit was disconnected? (AF3)**

Reflect

Invite the children to give an oral explanation of how a circuit works, using their own words. (AF2)

Task 4 Electrical Circuits

How an electrical circuit works

An electrical circuit is like a circle for electricity to travel around. Each part of the circuit is connected by wires. The electricity comes from a battery.

When the circuit is complete, electricity flows through the wires and into the bulb to make it light up.

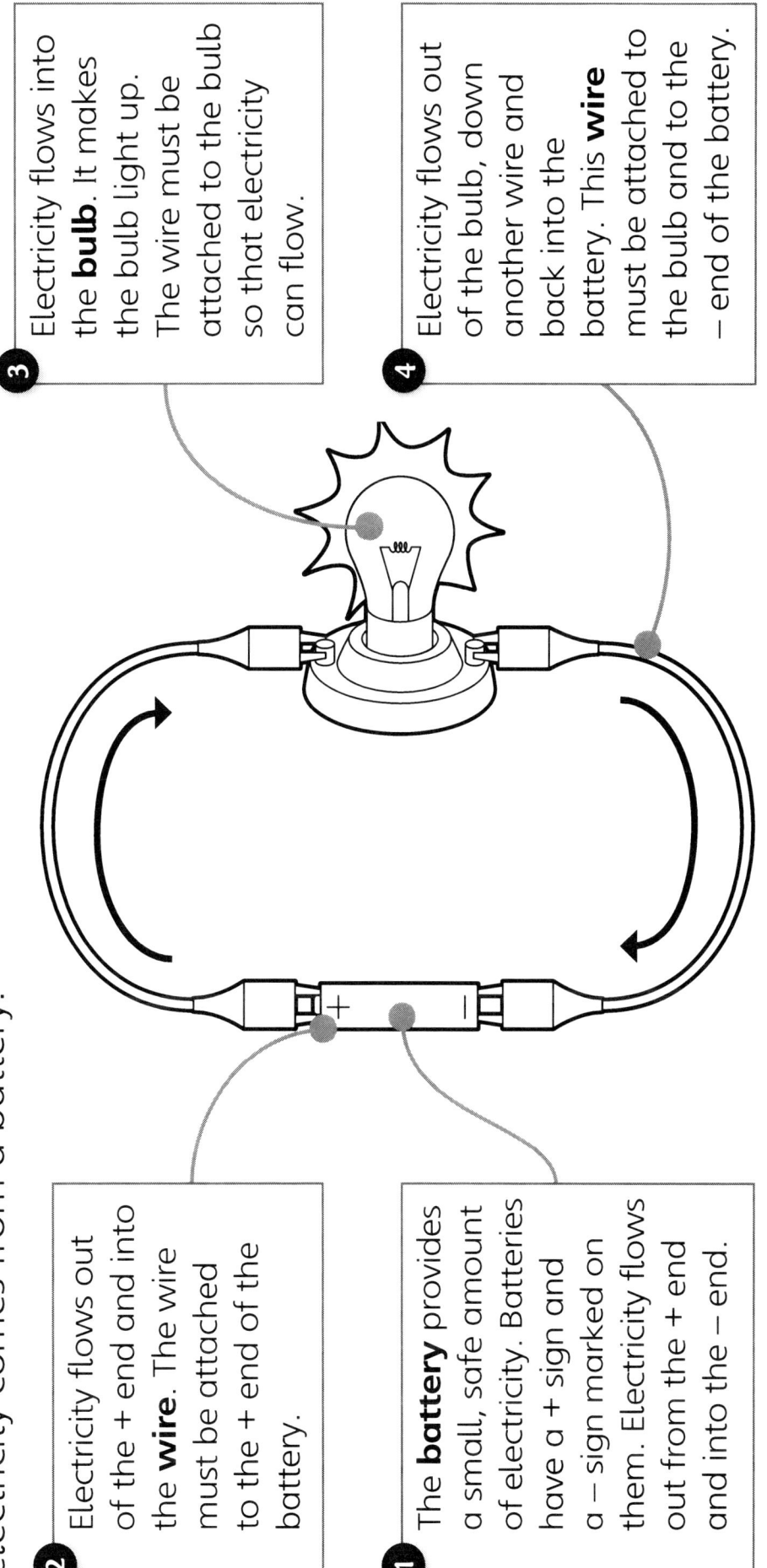

3 Electricity flows into the **bulb**. It makes the bulb light up. The wire must be attached to the bulb so that electricity can flow.

4 Electricity flows out of the bulb, down another wire and back into the battery. This **wire** must be attached to the bulb and to the – end of the battery.

2 Electricity flows out of the + end and into the **wire**. The wire must be attached to the + end of the battery.

1 The **battery** provides a small, safe amount of electricity. Batteries have a + sign and a – sign marked on them. Electricity flows out from the + end and into the – end.

Task 4 Electrical Circuits

1. What is an electrical circuit?

....

....

....

2a. After the introduction, where should you start to read?

....

2b. How do you know?

....

....

3. Why do batteries have a + and – sign on them?

....

....

....

© Pearson Education Ltd 2010. APP for Reading and Writing: Year 2

Task 4 Electrical Circuits

4. How does the diagram help to explain how a circuit works?

5. Why does the writer use the word 'flows' to describe the movement of electricity?

6. What do you think would happen if a wire in the circuit was disconnected?

If a wire in the circuit was disconnected

because

Task 4 Electrical Circuits

Main Assessment Focus: AF2 (understand, describe, select or retrieve information, events or ideas from texts and use quotation and reference to text)

Question	Exemplified responses	Grid reference	Notes
What is an electrical circuit?	Looks appropriately at opening paragraph for information; gives straightforward response, e.g. "It is a circle."	Level 2 / bullets 1 / 2	
	As above, but includes quotation, e.g. "It says it is like a circle for electricity to travel around."	Level 3 / bullets 1 / 2	
Why do batteries have a + and – sign on them?	Some information recalled, but not specific, e.g. "It's where the wires get attached."	Level 2 / bullet 1	
	Obvious points identified, but some misunderstanding of information, e.g. "It gives a + when the electricity goes into the wire and a – at the other end."	Level 3 / bullet 1	

Main Assessment Focus: AF3 (deduce, infer or interpret information, events or ideas from texts)

Question	Exemplified responses	Grid reference	Notes
What do you think would happen if a wire in the circuit was disconnected and why?	Makes a guess, e.g. "It might not work because it is broken."	Level 2 / bullet 1	
	Refers to the text, e.g. "It says the wire must be attached, so it wouldn't work because the electricity wouldn't flow any more."	Level 3 / bullet 1	

Main Assessment Focus: AF4 (identify and comment on the structure and organisation of texts, including grammatical and presentational features at text level)

Question	Exemplified responses	Grid reference	Notes
After the introduction, where should you start to read? How do you know?	Some awareness of paragraphs as a structural feature, but misses point of numbered explanation, e.g. "You should read the next paragraph."	Level 2	
	Able to identify numbering as a feature of text, e.g. "You need to read where it says 1 because that is the order."	Level 3	
How does the diagram help to explain how a circuit works?	Identifies the flow chart with a simple reason, e.g. "It has labels that tell you about how it works."	Level 2	
	Identifies the flow chart labels with an explanation about the language, e.g. "It tells you how the electricity flows through the wires and that they must be attached."	Level 3	

Main Assessment Focus: AF5 (explain and comment on writers' use of language, including grammatical and literary features at word and sentence level)

Question	Exemplified responses	Grid reference	Notes
Why does the writer use the word 'flows' to describe the movement of electricity?	Simple response, e.g. "Because it is a good word there."	Level 2 / bullet 1	
	Comment shows some awareness of writer's intent, e.g. "Because it makes electricity sound like water."	Level 3	

Exemplified responses matched to levels of attainment are provided as a guide. As always, professional judgement must be used when assessing pupils' learning progression and a range of evidence should be gathered for each AF.

Task 4 Electrical Circuits

1.

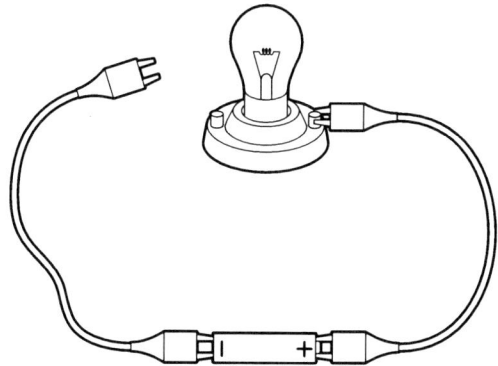

What is wrong with this circuit? Write a sentence.

2.

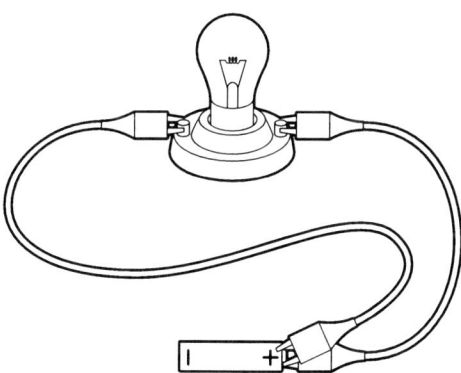

What is wrong with this circuit? Write a sentence.

3. Choose diagram 1 or 2 and write an explanation of how to make the circuit work.

Use the back of this sheet or a separate piece of paper.

Task 4 Electrical Circuits

A pupil response within the range for Level 2 might be:

Questions 1 and 2 (AF5, AF6, AF7)

- Uses simple sentences with 'and' to connect clauses, although 'because' might be used. Sentences demarcated accurately using capital letters and full stops. Some appropriate use of technical vocabulary:

  'The circuit is not right because the top wire is not connected to the bulb.'

  'The wire is not attached to the bulb and it is not a circle.'

Question 3 (AF3, AF5, AF6, AF7, AF8)

AF5
Use of simple connective: 'then'.
One long but clear sentence.
Inconsistency in tense.

AF6
Lacking in clause punctuation.
Use of capital letter at the beginning and full stop at the end.

AF7
Simple speech-like vocabulary relevant to the purpose and form.
Good use of appropriate technical words, e.g. 'circit', 'connect', 'battery', 'wire', 'bulb'.

AF3
Opening and closing signalled.
Shows basic sequence of information.

AF8
Mostly correct spelling.
Phonetic attempt at spelling 'coneced', which is successful at the end.

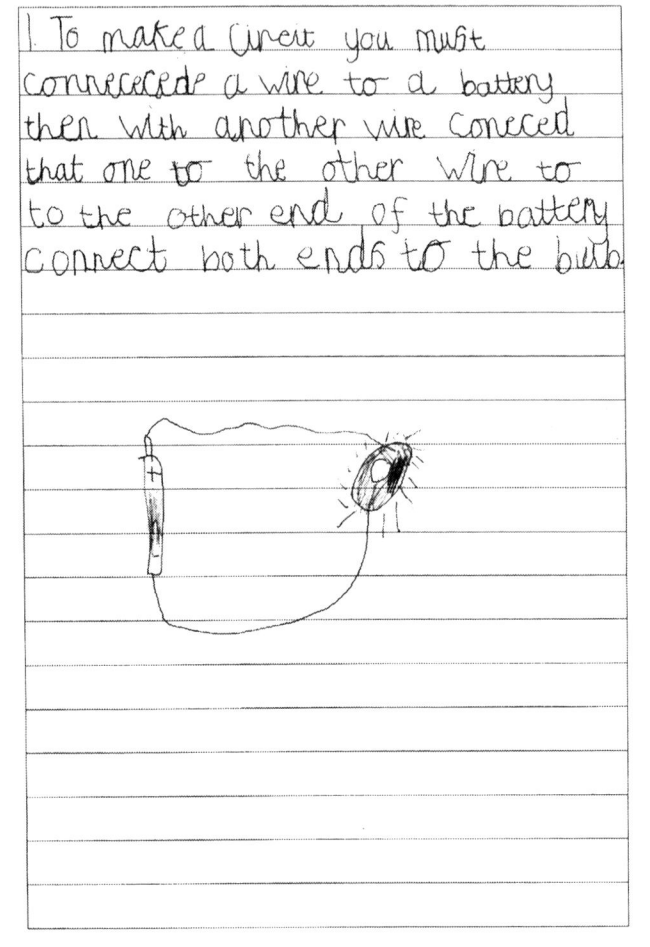

1. To make a circit you must conrececede a wire to a battery then with another wire coneced that one to the other wire to to the other end of the battery connect both ends to the bulb

Task 4 Electrical Circuits

A pupil response within the range for Level 3 might be:

Questions 1 and 2 (AF5, AF6, AF7)

• Evidence of use of causal connectives to join ideas in sentences (e.g. 'because', 'so', 'if'). Accurate use of capital letters and full stops most of the time. Appropriate use of technical vocabulary:

'The thing is that the top wire is not connected to the bulb, so the electricity can't flow into it.'

'Both the wires are attached to one end of the battery so that is why the circuit doesn't work.'

'It is wrong because both wires are in the same end of the battery and the bulb can't light up.'

'If the wires are attached at the same side of the battery it isn't a right circle.'

Question 3 (AF3, AF5, AF6, AF7, AF8)

AF5

Variation in sentence openings, e.g. 'To make a circuit ...'; 'A circuit is ...'; 'On the first ...'
The complex sentences are rather long and rambling, although the train of thought is mainly clear.
Use of active verb forms, e.g. 'If you pull ...'

AF6

Clause structure is poor and use of tenses confusing.
Lengthy sentences are mostly demarcated by capital letters and full stops, but no use of commas.

AF7

Deliberate vocabulary choices. Uses full array of technical words appropriate to the topic – 'battery', 'wires', 'bulb', 'circuit', 'circle' – including relevant verbs 'flows', 'atat' (attached).

> To make a circuit you will need o battry, wires, bulb to make it work if you do not have one of them it would not work. A circuit is a circle which flows electricity all the way around the circit and nether stops but if you pull it apat it will not work. On the first picher it will not work because the wires is not atat to the bulb so the bulb (this is wat) will not light up The circuit should look like after it has been finished if sav ⬡ but the first picher dose not show that so it has to be wrong.

AF8

Usually correct spelling.
Some phonetic attempts at more complex words, e.g. 'picher', 'battry', 'apat'.
'Nether' for 'never' reveals a pronunciation error.

AF3

Opening clearly signalled.
Shows an attempt to sequence the information using cause and effect vocabulary: 'but if', 'because', 'so'.

Task 4 Electrical Circuits

Reading

Next steps for developing AF2

Children will benefit from further practice in information retrieval from non-fiction texts by answering fact-based questions. Useful questions you could ask when reading a piece of non-fiction text together might be:

- What is the text about?
- Find 3 key facts about ….
- Where can you find out about …?

This activity should be part of a range of evidence gathered for AF2. Evidence for AF2 can be gathered from a range of sources, such as:

- observations during guided and shared reading;
- finding information from other sources, such as maps, diagrams etc;
- research in other subject areas, e.g. finding information in geography.

Tasks 5 and 6 on pages 52 to 72 provide other opportunities to gather evidence for AF2 when reading non-fiction.

Next steps for developing AF3

Children will benefit from further practice in interpreting the information in information texts. Questions you could ask to stimulate thought include:

- Does the text answer all your questions? If not, which questions doesn't it answer? Where could you go to find out the answers to those questions?
- What can you tell about … from this chart / photograph / diagram?
- What does … [word / phrase] mean?

This activity should be part of a range of evidence gathered for AF3. Evidence for AF3 can be gathered from a range of sources, such as:

- observations during guided and shared reading;
- comparing information in different texts on the same subject;
- asking children to interpret information by presenting it in a different format.

Task 5 on pages 52 to 62 is another opportunity to gather evidence for AF3 when reading non-fiction.

Next steps for developing AF4

Children will benefit from further practice in understanding how information texts are structured and organised and how this helps readers find and understand the information. Questions you could ask when reading non-fiction texts include:

- Where would you look to find out about …?
- How important is the order of information in the whole text?
- What does the diagram tell you about …?

This activity should be part of a range of evidence gathered for AF4. Evidence for AF4 can be gathered from a range of sources, such as:

- observations during guided and shared reading;
- searching for information in books, multi-modal texts and on the internet;
- classroom discussions about information texts;
- sequencing and sorting jumbled pictures, lines, sentences or paragraphs from a text;
- planning their own non-fiction text and explaining their decisions.

Task 6 on pages 63 to 72 is another opportunity to gather evidence for AF4.

Task 4 Electrical Circuits

Reading (continued)

Next steps for developing AF5

To develop children's ability to explain and comment on why particular words are used, read a range of non-fiction texts to and with them and talk about the words:

- Are some words more important than others? Why?
- What kinds of words are useful in instruction writing?

This activity should be part of a range of evidence gathered for AF5. Evidence for AF5 can be gathered from a range of sources, such as:

- observations during shared and guided reading;
- responses to visual images;
- speaking and listening activities;
- simple text-marking activities.

Task 2 on pages 21 to 29 is another opportunity to gather evidence for AF5.

Writing

Next steps for developing AF5

In order to progress children's ability to write clear and varied sentences in non-fiction texts, pupils should be given:

- practice in writing complex sentences using causal connectives, such as *If... then*, and in joining clauses using *because*;
- opportunities for oral practice, e.g. 'human' sentence activities.

This activity should be part of a range of evidence gathered for AF5, such as Task 6 on pages 63 to 72.

Next steps for developing AF6

In order to progress children's ability to write using accurate grammar and punctuation, it is helpful if they have plenty of opportunities to:

- explore how this is used in well-written text during shared and guided reading;
- explore how meaning can be affected by inaccurate use.

This activity should be part of a range of evidence gathered for AF6, such as Task 1 on pages 9 to 20 and Task 5 on pages 52 to 62.

Next steps for developing AF7

In order to progress children's ability to use technical and precise vocabulary in non-fiction writing, give them opportunities to:

- write in other curriculum areas such as history, geography and science;
- make and use personal collections of words and phrases from their reading in other curriculum areas, which will help to build up their store of words and their ability to use them effectively.

This activity should be part of a range of evidence gathered for AF7. All the tasks in this book provide opportunities to gather such evidence.

Task 5 Allan Ahlberg

Aims of this task
This task is designed to help you make judgements about children's performance in Reading **AF2**, and **AF3** (with opportunities to assess AF1 and AF4 as well), and Writing **AF2**, **AF6** and **AF7** (with opportunities to assess AF1 and AF8 as well). Children read and respond to a short information text about some of the books of children's author, Allan Ahlberg. They write a book review of their own.

Related Renewed Framework unit
Non-fiction Unit 3: Information texts

Renewed Framework objectives
5.2, 7.1, 7.3, 8.3, 9.3, 9.4, 11.1

Key concepts
Reading
- find specific information by referring to the text (AF2)
- deduce the content of the books (AF3)
- understand the purpose of features in the text (AF4)

Writing
- write sentences appropriate for a book review (AF2)
- use simple punctuation accurately and write grammatically correct sentences (AF6)
- use some interesting vocabulary to engage the reader (AF7)

Questions for guided reading

Starting off
If possible, before the session, make a collection of books by Allan Ahlberg. Ask the children if they know who Allan Ahlberg is. Explain that he is a well-known author of children's books. Have they ever read any of his books? Explain that they are going to read an information text describing some of Allan Ahlberg's books. Point out any new or unusual vocabulary (such as 'hilarious') and discuss the meanings before asking the children to read. (AF1)

Read and respond
Check that the children have understood the text, using the following questions:
- **Which book has surprises hidden in it? (AF2)**
- **Which book is funny? How do you know? (AF2)**
- **Which books might contain rhyming words? Why do you think that? (AF3)**
- **Has anyone else contributed to the books? How do you know? (AF2)**

Going deeper
- **What does the front cover of *Funnybones* tell you about the book? (AF3)**
- **Why do you think the text includes photographs? (AF4)**
- What sort of information does the text give you about each book? (AF3)

Reflect
Invite the children to think about the order in which the books are detailed. Do they think a different order would change the text? (AF4)

Task 5 Allan Ahlberg

Allan Ahlberg

Allan Ahlberg writes books for children of all ages. Have you read any of his books?

Very young children love the pictures and rhymes in *Each Peach Pear Plum*.

Task 5 Allan Ahlberg

The Jolly Postman is an amazing book. It has letters and all sorts of surprises hidden in it. Children of all ages enjoy reading it.

Funnybones is a hilarious book about skeletons. Children from 5 to 8 years old love hearing it or reading it by themselves.

Children aged 7 to 11 love Allan Ahlberg's poems about school in *Please Mrs Butler*.

Allan Ahlberg is writing new books all the time...

Task 5 Allan Ahlberg

1. Which book has surprises hidden in it?

2. Which book is funny? How do you know?

3a. Which books might contain rhyming words?

3b. Why do you think that?

I think that because

4. Has anyone else contributed to the books? How do you know?

Task 5 Allan Ahlberg

5. Why do you think the text includes photographs?

6. What does the front cover of *Funnybones* tell you about the book?

Task 5 Allan Ahlberg

Main Assessment Focus: AF2 (understand, describe, select or retrieve information, events or ideas from texts and use quotation and reference to texts)

Question	Exemplified responses	Grid reference	Notes
Which book has surprises hidden in it?	Straightforward information recalled or located with prompting, e.g. "The Jolly Postman".	Level 2 / bullet 1	
	Information identified with quotation from text, e.g. "It says The Jolly Postman has all sorts of surprises hidden in it."	Level 3 / bullet 2	
Which book is funny? How do you know?	Straightforward information given, sometimes with prompting, e.g. "Funnybones because it has funny in the title."	Level 2 / bullet 1	
	Straightforward information given with reference to both book title as above and book description, e.g. "Funnybones because it has funny in the title and it says the book is hilarious."	Level 3 / bullets 1 / 2	
Has anyone else contributed to the books? How do you know?	With prompting, is able to recognise 'Janet and Allan Ahlberg' on covers.	Level 2 / bullet 2	
	Without prompting, identifies the information on the book covers. May include speculation, e.g. "Maybe Janet Ahlberg did the pictures."	Level 3 / bullet 2	

Main Assessment Focus: AF3 (deduce, infer or interpret information, events and ideas from texts)

Which books might contain rhyming words? Why do you think that?	Uses 'rhymes' in the book description of *Each Peach Pear Plum* to identify one book.	Level 2 / bullet 1	
	Suggests *Each Peach Pear Plum* and *Please Mrs Butler* "because the poems might rhyme too".	Level 3 / bullet 1	
What does the front cover of *Funnybones* tell you about the book?	Identifies the title, author and main characters from the cover.	Level 2 / bullet 1	
	Some further detail inferred from the cover, e.g. "It is about 2 skeletons and a dog at night."	Level 3 / bullet 1	

Other Assessment Focus: AF4 (identify and comment on the structure and organisation of texts, including grammatical and literary features at word and sentence level)

Why do you think there are illustrations in the text?	Straightforward literal response, e.g. "to show you what they look like".	Level 2 / bullet 1	
	Some awareness of the effect of the text's overall organisation and presentation, e.g. "It makes it more interesting to read."	Level 3 / bullet 1	

Exemplified responses matched to levels of attainment are provided as a guide. As always, professional judgement must be used when assessing pupils' learning progression and a range of evidence should be gathered for each AF.

Task 5 Allan Ahlberg

Write a book review of your favourite book.

Book title: ....

Author ....

What is the book about?

....

....

....

What is the best bit of the book? Why?

....

....

....

What is the worst bit? Why?

....

....

....

Who else would enjoy this book? Why?

....

....

....

Task 5 Allan Ahlberg

A pupil response within the range for Level 2 might be:

AF2

Clear sentences that suit the purpose, although detail about the book is sparse.

Good overview of book in response to 'What is the book about?'

AF6

Uses full stops correctly most of the time. Capital letters used correctly for the book title, author's name, and for personal pronoun 'I', but omits them in the other sentences (e.g. 'everyone', 'when').

Write a book review of your favourite book.

Book title: Helpful Hannah

Author Marie Burlington

What is the book about? Only evryone dose not like K Hannah but then she started to be Helpful and evryone started to like her.

What is the best bit of the book? Why? I like were where evryone starts to like Hannah. because I like happy things.

What is the worst bit? Why? when everyone dose not like her because I don not like sad parts of any storys

Who else would enjoy this book? Why? Alex because I fun thinke Alex likes jobs.

AF8

Generally correct spelling. Makes plausible attempts at polysyllabic words, e.g. 'evryone', and corrects it later.
Error in inflected plural 'storys'.

AF1

Supports comments about the book with statements of personal opinion and viewpoint: 'I do not like sad parts of any story.'

AF7

Chooses simple vocabulary appropriate for a book review with a good summary of the book.

Task 5 Allan Ahlberg

A pupil response within the range for Level 3 might be:

AF2
Clearly written and suited for the purpose.
The 'why?' questions consistently and appropriately answered.

AF6
Although answers are not in complete sentences, clauses and phrases are mostly grammatically correct with accurate use of capital letters and full stops.
Lack of apostrophes in contractions ('whos', 'hed').

Write a book review of your favourite book.

Book title: _A pipRin of pepper_

Author _Helen Cooper_

What is the book about? _Three animals that make pumkin soup but they ran out of salt so they go to the big city but the little duck gets lost. But the cat and the squirel find him._

What is the best bit of the book? Why? _When they ride on the helecopter because I like helecopters._

What is the worst bit? Why? _When the duck gets lost because he feels very scared._

Who else would enjoy this book? Why? _My littel brother whos two hed like the helecopter_

AF8
Mostly accurate spelling with good attempt at polysyllabic word 'helecopters' and phonetically plausible spelling of unstressed syllable in 'littel' (little).

AF1
Clear personal reflection.
Supports statements about the book with own opinion and the story character's opinion: '... he feels very scared'.

AF7
Some vocabulary chosen to engage readers' interest, e.g. '... but the little duck gets lost'.
Some words chosen for effect, e.g. 'helecopters', 'very scared'.

Task 5 Allan Ahlberg

Reading

Next steps for developing AF2

Children will benefit from further practice in information retrieval by answering fact-based questions. Useful questions you could ask when reading a piece of information text together might be:

• What is the information text about?

• What new thing(s) did you find out about …?

• Where can you find information about …?

• What is the main idea in this section / paragraph?

This activity should be part of a range of evidence gathered for AF2. Evidence for AF2 can be gathered from a range of sources, such as:

• observations during guided and shared reading;

• finding information in other formats, such as maps and diagrams, and from other media, such as websites and television;

• reading for information in other subject areas, e.g. science, history, geography.

Task 1 on pages 9 to 20, Tasks 3 and 4 on pages 30–51 and Task 6 on pages 63 to 72 all provide other opportunities to gather evidence for AF2.

Next steps for developing AF3

Children will benefit from further practice in interpreting the information in information texts. Questions you could ask to stimulate thought include:

• Does the text answer all your questions? If not, which questions doesn't it answer? Where could you go to find out the answers to those questions?

• What can you tell about … from this chart / photograph / diagram?

• What does … [word / phrase] mean?

This activity should be part of a range of evidence gathered for AF3. Evidence for AF3 can be gathered from a range of sources, such as:

• observations during guided and shared reading;

• comparing information in different texts on the same subject;

• asking children to interpret information by presenting it in a different format.

Task 1 on pages 9 to 20 and Task 4 on pages 42 to 51 provide other opportunities to gather evidence for AF3.

Next steps for developing AF4

Children will benefit from further practice in understanding the structure and organisation of texts and how these affect their ability to retrieve information. Questions you could ask include:

• What is the difference between fiction and non-fiction?

• How do you know where to go to find information about …?

• How does the writer help you to find the information you need?

• Why has the writer included a diagram / photograph / chart?

This activity should be part of a range of evidence gathered for AF4. Evidence for A4 can be gathered from a range of sources, such as:

• observations during guided and shared reading;

• activities requiring sequencing and re-formatting jumbled up texts;

• discussion about how different texts are organised and presented.

Task 4 on pages 42 to 51 and Task 6 on pages 63 to 72 provide other opportunities to gather evidence for AF4.

Task 5 Allan Ahlberg

Writing

Next steps for developing AF2

In order to progress children's ability to write information texts, pupils should be:

- given opportunities to choose subject matter that interests them;
- encouraged to use their knowledge of text-types to decide on structure and form;
- encouraged to edit and improve their own and others' work, e.g. cutting out and reordering information, or grouping information in more adventurous ways to benefit their own writing.

This activity should be part of a range of evidence gathered for AF2, such as Tasks 2 and 3 on pages 21 to 41.

Next steps for developing AF6

In order to progress children's ability to write using accurate grammar and punctuation, it is helpful if they have plenty of opportunities to:

- explore how this is used in well-written text during shared and guided reading;
- explore how meaning can be affected by inaccurate use of grammar and punctuation;
- think aloud how to use punctuation to support meaning and create effects, e.g. 'Now I want to ask a question, to hook the reader in. *What was it?* I need to use a question mark to make the reader aware that it is a question.'
- identify sentences from their own writing to be improved, and amend them verbally and in writing.

This activity should be part of a range of evidence gathered for AF6, such as Task 1 on pages 9 to 20 and Task 4 on pages 42 to 51.

Next steps for developing AF7

In order to progress children's ability to use technical and precise vocabulary in non-fiction writing, give them opportunities to:

- use speaking and listening activities to describe with precision an object, animal or person;
- write in other curriculum areas such as history, geography and science;
- make and use personal collections of words and phrases from their reading in other curriculum areas, which will help to build up their store of words and their ability to use them effectively.

This activity should be part of a range of evidence gathered for AF7. All the tasks in this book provide opportunities to gather such evidence.

Task 6 Birds in the City

Aims of this task

This task is designed to help you make judgements about children's performance in Reading **AF2**, **AF4** and **AF6** (with opportunity to assess AF1 as well) and Writing **AF3**, **AF4** and **AF5** (with opportunities to assess AF6 and AF7 as well). Children read and respond to a short non-chronological report text about birds that live in cities. Then, using notes provided, they write about two other city birds.

Related Renewed Framework unit

Non-fiction Unit 4: Non-chronological reports

Renewed Framework objectives

7.1, 7.3, 9.3, 9.5, 10.1, 11.2

Key concepts

Reading
- retrieve and understand specific information from the text (AF2)
- identify and comment on the organisational features of the text (AF4)
- understand the purpose of the text (AF6)

Writing
- structure and organise information into paragraphs (AF3 and AF4)
- use appropriate tense and sentence structure (AF5)

Questions for guided reading

Starting off

Show the children the Resource Sheet. Ask the children: Is this a fiction or a non-fiction text? How do you know? Read and discuss the title. What information can they discover from the title?

Point out any new or unusual vocabulary (e.g. *countryside, buildings, warmth, flocks*) and discuss the meanings before asking the children to read. (AF1)

Read and respond

Check that the children have understood the text, using the following questions:
- **Find three reasons why birds move into cities. (AF2)**
- **Which types of birds live in towns and cities? (AF2)**
- **What is the purpose of this text? How do you know? (AF6)**
- **Why does the book have an index? (AF4)**
- On which page of the book would you find information about sparrows? (AF2)
- Information on which birds might also tell you something about worms? (AF3)

Going deeper

- **Who do think might want to read a book about birds in the city? (AF6)**
- **What sort of information is given about both pigeons and starlings? How is this information organised to help you find the information? (AF4)**
- Look at the photograph in the bottom left of the page. Read the caption. What information do the photograph and caption add to the text? (AF4)
- Find the nouns in the text. Are they singular or plural nouns? Can you give a reason for this? (AF4)
- Why do you think the information about pigeons comes before the information about starlings? (AF4)

Reflect

Invite the children to suggest other texts they have read that use a similar way of giving information to readers. (AF7)

Task 6 Birds in the City

Birds in the city

Introduction

When we think about where birds live, we often think of the countryside or the seaside. But many different kinds of birds live in crowded, noisy towns and cities.

A flock of pigeons in a city square.

Some birds move into cities in search of food and a safe place to make their home. Some birds move into cities during the winter months for warmth.

Birds clean up the pavement. They eat food dropped by people!

Types of city birds

Pigeons

Pigeons live in most towns and cities. They nest on buildings high above the ground. Pigeons can be seen in city centre squares and market places. They often eat food that people drop.

A hole in a building makes a perfect nest.

Starlings

Starlings are very common in city centres during winter. They build their nests in trees or holes in buildings such as lofts or attics. In the evening, they gather in huge flocks. Starlings eat almost anything.

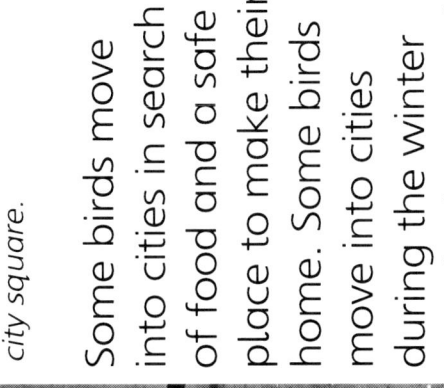

A starling in London.

Index

birds of prey	13
blackbirds	14
ducks	15
magpies	16
pigeons	17
robins	18
starlings	20
sparrows	21
water	17
worms	14, 18

Task 6 Birds in the City

1. Find three reasons why birds move into cities.

   1. ....

   2. ....

   3. ....

2. Which types of birds live in town and cities?

3a. What is the purpose of this text?

3b. How do you know?

© Pearson Education Ltd 2010. APP for Reading and Writing: Year 2

Task 6 Birds in the City

4. Why does the book have an index?

5. Who do you think might want to read a book about birds in the city?

6a. What sort of information is given about both pigeons and starlings?

6b. How is this information organised to help you find the information?

Task 6 Birds in the City

Main Assessment Focus: AF2 (understand, describe, select or retrieve information, events or ideas from texts and use quotation and reference to texts)

Question	Exemplified responses	Grid reference	Notes
Find three reasons why birds move into cities.	At least two reasons recalled without prompting, e.g. "Food and a safe place."	Level 2 / bullet 1	
	Three reasons identified and may include quotation or reference to text, e.g. "To get food, a safe place to make their home / nests, to get warm."	Level 3 / bullets 1 / 2	
What types of birds live in towns and cities?	Simply identifies the two birds written about – i.e. pigeons and starlings.	Level 2 / bullets 1 / 2	
	Uses the 'index' to identify other birds – e.g. blackbirds, magpies, robins, sparrows, birds of prey.	Level 3 / bullets 1 / 2	

Main Assessment Focus: AF4 (identify and comment on the structure and organisation of texts, including grammatical and presentational features at text level)

Question	Exemplified responses	Grid reference	Notes
Why does the book have an index?	Shows some awareness of the purpose, e.g. "It tells you which pages different things are on."	Level 2 / bullet 1	
	Shows awareness of the purpose, e.g. "You can quickly find pages with the information you want to read about."	Level 3 / bullet 1	
What sort of information is given about pigeons and starlings?	May identify some of four different areas of information (where they live, where they build nests, what they eat, what they do) and suggest 'headings' as an organisational feature.	Level 2 / bullet 1	
How is this information organised to help you find the information?	Identifies areas of information; may also recognise the pattern of information in each paragraph under 'Types of city birds' and comment on how it helps you find information quickly, e.g. "You can skim over the page and find things."	Level 3 / bullet 1	

Main Assessment Focus: AF6 (identify and comment on writers' purposes and viewpoints, and the overall effect of the text on the reader)

Question	Exemplified responses	Grid reference	Notes
What is the purpose of this text? How do you know?	Simple statement, e.g. "It tells you about birds. I know because it says so in the text."	Level 2 / bullet 1	
	Simple statement with further detail, e.g. "It tells you about birds that live in cities. It starts by saying we think about birds in the countryside and goes on to give information about city birds."	Level 3 / bullet 1	
Who do you think might want to read a book about birds in the city?	Shows some awareness of audience, but confuses 'who' with 'why', e.g. "To find out about birds in the city."	Level 2 / bullet 1	
	Shows awareness of audience and may give a specific audience, e.g. "A child who wants to know which birds are in cities."	Level 3 / bullet 1	

Exemplified responses matched to levels of attainment are provided as a guide. As always, professional judgement must be used when assessing pupils' learning progression and a range of evidence should be gathered for each AF.

Task 6 Birds in the City

Here are some notes about two other city birds.

Robins		Magpies
worms, seeds, fruit and insects	**Nests**	scavenge and eat almost anything
sing at night next to street lights	**What they eat**	large nests in tall trees and even pylons
often nest in containers in city gardens	**What they do**	becoming more common in cities today

1. Draw lines from the notes to the headings they belong with.

2. Write a caption for this picture of a robin's nest.

....

....

....

3. Use the notes about robins and magpies.
   Write two new paragraphs for the book about birds in the city.
   Use a separate piece of paper.

   REMEMBER!

   - Use headings and sub-headings.

   - Include a picture and a caption.

Task 6 Birds in the City

A pupil response within the range for Level 2 might be:

Question 1 (AF4)
- Most notes are linked with relevant heading, but there may be confusion about where to place those notes that don't have clues in the words, e.g. 'sing at night next to street lights' and 'becoming more common in cities today'.

Question 2 (AF5)
- Caption is simple sentence, though may not always use the present tense appropriately. Content may not be precisely relevant:

  'Robins live in any where such as garden pots.'

  'Robins find holes in the wall.'

Question 3 (AF3, AF4, AF5, AF6, AF7)

AF3

Ideas organised in sections based on the model text in a logical sequence with related points.

No use of sub-headings (i.e. Robins, Magpies) or picture captions.

AF4

Ideas written in sections.

Sentences linked by use of simple pronoun 'they'.

AF5

Uses simple sentences.

Varied sentence openings starting with name, e.g. 'Robins', or simple pronoun 'They'.

Uses appropriate tense consistently.

AF6

Capital letters and full stops used accurately and consistently.

AF7

Appropriate vocabulary taken from notes made.

Vocabulary use is suited to the type of text.

Robins and magpeis

Robins eat worms, seeds, fruit and insects. They often nest in containers. Robins sing at night. They live in city. Robins eat food is the ground that peple have dropped

Magpies almost eat anything. They nest in tall trees and pylons. Magpia are becoming more common in cities. They also live in citys to.

Task 6 Birds in the City

A pupil response within the range for Level 3 might be:

Question 1 (AF4)
- Notes linked appropriately with relevant heading, showing awareness of how ideas are grouped by content.

Question 2 (AF5)
- Relevant caption using present tense; may elaborate to add extra information:

  'A robin's nest needs leaves and green grass.'

  'Robins like to sleep in flower pots. They like to keep warm.'

Question 3 (AF3, AF4, AF5, AF6, AF7)

AF3
Ideas are clearly organised by related points.

No use of sub-headings (i.e. Robins, Magpies) or picture captions.

AF4
Distinct sections with paragraphs within the sections linked by use of simple pronoun 'They'.

AF5
Varied sentence structure with sentences beginning with the name and simple pronoun 'They'.

Clauses connected using 'but' and 'because', showing cause and effect.

Elaborates on the basic information with added detail: 'gardens are better homes for them because…'; 'those trees are tall'.

AF6
Accurate use of capital letters and full stops. Uses commas in a list.

AF7
Vocabulary chosen for variety and effect, e.g. 'rumege' (rummage).

Robins and Magpies

Robins can eat worms, seeds, fruit, vegetables and insects.

They come into gardens and citys, but gardens are better homes for them because they are quiter.

They also sing alot in citys and gardens at night.

Magpies are into gold and jelrey.

They rumege on the ground for food and eat nearly anything.

They normely rest in trees that are in citys and those trees are tall.

Shu Shop

Task 6 Birds in the City

Reading

Next steps for developing AF2

Children will benefit from further practice in information retrieval by answering fact-based questions. Useful questions you could ask when reading a piece of non-chronological report text together might be:

- What is the text about?
- What do you already know about ...?
- What new thing(s) did you find out about ...?
- Where can you find information about ...?

This activity should be part of a range of evidence gathered for AF2. Evidence for AF2 can be gathered from a range of sources, such as:

- observations during guided and shared reading;
- finding information in other formats, such as maps and diagrams, and from other media, such as websites and television;
- reading for information in other subject areas, e.g. science, history, geography.

Task 1 on pages 9 to 20 and Tasks 3, 4 and 5 on pages 30 to 62 provide other opportunities to gather evidence for AF2.

Next steps for developing AF4

Children will benefit from having opportunities to discuss whole texts in terms of how they are organised and structured and the impact of this, using text with varying layouts and features. Questions you could ask to stimulate thought include:

- How do the contents page and / or index help readers?
- Why does the text use diagrams?
- Would the text make sense if the sequence were different?
- What is the quickest way to find out about ...?

This activity should be part of a range of evidence gathered for AF4. Evidence for A4 can be gathered from a range of sources, such as:

- observations during guided and shared reading;
- searching for information in books, multi-modal texts and on the internet;
- classroom discussions about information texts;
- sequencing and sorting jumbled pictures, sentences or paragraphs from a text.

Task 4 on pages 42 to 51 is another opportunity to gather evidence for AF4.

Next steps for developing AF6

Children will benefit from further practice in understanding the purpose of non-fiction texts and the overall effect through classroom discussion in shared and guided reading. Questions you could ask to stimulate thought include:

- What is the purpose of this text?
- Who would want to read this text?
- Did you find the information in the text useful?

This activity should be part of a range of evidence gathered for AF6. Evidence for A6 can be gathered from a range of sources, such as:

- observations during guided and shared reading;
- classroom discussions about information texts;
- comparing different non-fiction texts on the same subject.

Task 2 on pages 21 to 29 is another opportunity to gather evidence for AF6

Task 6 Birds in the City

Writing

Next steps for developing AF3

In order to progress children's ability to organise information effectively and appropriately for the purpose, pupils should be given opportunities to:

- in shared and guided reading sessions, explore how writers link and sequence events and ideas;
- choose subject matter that interests them;
- use their knowledge of text-types to decide on structure and form;
- edit and improve their own and others' work by, for example, cutting out and reordering information, or grouping information in more adventurous ways.

This activity should be part of a range of evidence gathered for AF3, such as Tasks 2 and 3 on pages 21 to 41.

Next steps for developing AF4

In order to progress children's ability to write in paragraphs and group information logically and effectively, it is helpful if they have:

- opportunities to explore how paragraphs are structured and linked in well-written texts during shared and guided reading;
- time for planning their own non-fiction texts, using writing scaffolds, flow charts etc;
- writing partners with whom they can share and explain their decisions before writing.

This activity should be part of a range of evidence gathered for AF4.

Next steps for developing AF5

In order to progress children's ability to write with clarity in non-fiction writing, give them opportunities to:

- practise using a wider range of connectives to create complex sentences with subordination;
- explore varied sentence structures in activities such as human sentences, and cutting out and reordering clauses and phrases;
- re-write text from present to past tense and vice-versa and discuss the effect;
- write in other curriculum areas such as history, geography and science.

This activity should be part of a range of evidence gathered for AF5, such as Task 4 on pages 42 to 51.